I CAME.
I SAW.
I JUMPED!

I CAME.
I SAW.
I JUMPED!

How I found my dream job and you can too!

Petros Eshetu

Inspired Mind Publishing

Copyright © 2017 by Petros Eshetu

All rights reserved. This book or any portion thereof may not be reproduced or used in any manner whatsoever without the express written permission of the publisher; however, brief quotations may be used in a book review. For more information, please contact petros@petroseshetu.com

Printed in the United States of America

First Printing, 2017

ISBN 978-0-9985548-0-8

This publication is designed to provide accurate and authoritative information with regard to the subject matter covered. It is sold with the understanding that the publisher is not engaged in rendering legal, accounting or other professional advice. If legal advice or other expert assistance is required, the services of a competent professional should be sought. Petros Eshetu individually or corporately does not accept any responsibility for any liabilities that result from the actions of any parties.

Inspired Mind Publishing

Table of Contents

INTRODUCTION 1
- Life: When you zig, it zags. 3
- Reaching a crossroads 5
- The million-dollar question: What do I want? 7
- Making a U-turn 7
- The distance to the top 9
- Promises 11
- Begin Now 13

CHAPTER 1 15

LIFE IS TOO SHORT TO BE A CORPORATE SLAVE 15
- A serial job hopper 16
- Emancipation and the straw that broke the camel's back 18
- Who am I? What steps did I take to get here? 20
- The journey 23
- On life's regrets 24
- The #1 killer of dreams is procrastination. 27

CHAPTER 2 31

PURPOSE AND PASSION 31
- Family culture- Escaping the established form of government 32
- Generational Differences 33
- What is my passion? 35
- How do I select a passion if I have so many? 36
- 3 Step Formula to Fulfillment 38

CHAPTER 3 57

THE TRUTH ABOUT TASTING COURAGE 57
- Knowing when to jump? 58
- Who am I, if not me? 59
- D-day; quitting 61
- No schedule; what to do today? 64
- Tempted by a 30% salary increase 66
- Quitter myth 68

CHAPTER 4 71

HAND AND FOOT PLACEMENT- YOU DO NOT WANT TO FALL TO YOUR DEATH- THE ABC PLAN 71

- JUMPING WITHOUT PARACHUTE 71
- ABC IS AS EASY, AS 1-2-3 75
- GO BIG OR GO HOME 88
- CHANGING IDENTITIES 89
- RE-INVENT YOURSELF. 90

CHAPTER 5 95

DO NOT LET OTHERS KEEP YOU AT THE BOTTOM OF THE MOUNTAIN. 95

- YOUR SUPPORTERS 96
- COMPADRES 98
- BIRDS OF A FEATHER, FLOCK TOGETHER 100
- AS THE SEASONS CHANGE, SO DO YOUR RELATIONSHIPS 101
- PAIN FUELS YOUR SUCCESS 103

CHAPTER 6 109

IF IT DIDN'T KILL YOU, THEN IT'S TIME TO LIVE; CREATING GOALS AND VISIONS 109

- A SPARROW OR AN EAGLE 111
- COMPLETE YOUR VISION 116

CHAPTER 7 127

BREAKING LOOSE, NEVER LOOKING BACK AND EMBRACING A MINDSET OF FREEDOM 127

- WHAT MAKES YOU SWEAT? 131
- THE MIND TRAP 131
- MENTAL PROGRAMS WE DOWNLOADED 133
- FINDS THE WEEDS IN THE MIND 135
- WHAT TUNE IS RUNNING YOUR SHOW? 136
- GET COMFORTABLE BEING UNCOMFORTABLE 139

CHAPTER 8 143

LANDING ON YOUR FEET AND HOW TO STAY THERE; CLEARING TECHNIQUES .. 143

- CLEARING 145
- AWARENESS- BEING AWARE OF THE MIND TRAP, A SLAVE AT HEART 147
- MANTRA-REPEAT IT TILL YOU BELIEVE IT 151

Time management	156
Gratitude is an attitude	158
Visualization	160
How to create a vision board	162
Drawing	163
Motivational Poster	167

CONCLUSION **171**

REFERENCES **185**

Acknowledgements

I dedicate this book firstly to my "mum," who has always supported me to follow my dreams. Her encouragement and belief in me, even when it was not popular amongst family and friends led to my improved focus, and to the achievement of my goals. I would not be where I am today without her guidance and unwavering support.

The love of my life, Lisa, my wife has been a rock of support. I am so grateful. There were many times when I almost gave up, and somehow, she would always come with a message to keep me going. When I was in pursuit of a dream, she was alongside cheering me on. When we were in college, she worked at two or more jobs while I focused on getting my MBA. Even when I quit my job during my transition, she stepped in to keep us afloat.

I want to thank all of my family and friends for the support throughout this project. Encouragement from phone conversations, texts or emails gave me the boost of energy I needed to move forward. I am so grateful for having all of you in my life. Shout to my brother Paul for being my 2nd pair of ears when listening to my ideas and always giving me straight honest feedback on whether my ideas sucked or were great. Also, big shout out to Samson for being not only my 2nd pair of eyes but also being my first editor in helping review this book, providing invaluable advice.

Most of all with deep sincerity, I thank the *Achieve Today* organization for helping me in my life transformation. Not only did I learn to remove the mental obstacles that had held me back for many years, but I also learned to dream big and not to be afraid to pursue my goals. I learned to take action every day toward my dream, and not to accept things as they are. I am thankful for all of the resources they gave; coaches, videos, retreats, etc.

I want to give a shout out to my coach, Aisake at *Achieve Today*, who helped me start my transformation to be the person that I always knew I was. Aisake's positive energy always pushed me forward to take on challenges. I learned many strategies and lessons in our meetings that have helped me overcome many of my challenges. These are life lessons that I still apply as part of my daily routine. I want to thank my other powerful coach, Rainbow, for her leadership, wisdom, and feedback. Rainbow's encouragement, honesty, and creativity were invaluable in making this book the best that it can be. I have become a better writer under her guidance.

Finally, I want to express my greatest gratitude to Dr. Joe Vitale for creating both the Miracle coaching program and the Authorship program (through Achieve Today). Having a Miracle's coach by my side has been such a big influence in my turnaround that I do not recognize the person I was a few months ago. I have made more progress in the last five months than I had made in the last five years. I am so grateful for Joe and the whole Achieve Today organization and the benefits I have received.

I came. I saw. I jumped!

INTRODUCTION

Twelve-years-old, palms sweaty and knees weak, I stood at the base of the boulder. My courage diminishing, I strapped on my climbing harness and stared at the national park rock which had already won the battle in my mind. I did not want to climb it, but I knew I had to. After all, the climbers were all lined up, and I was next. I heard the instructor call my name again, his voice echoing in my mind. On top of the boulder, another instructor waved the go-ahead for the next kid to climb. Even though I was feeling the pressure of holding up the line, there was only one thing I could do: Grab the rough stone and climb!

Reaching up, I grasped the harsh surface of the boulder. I felt a warm trickle of blood swirl down my shin. I had scraped my leg against the rock. Sweat dotted my face, but I did not dare wipe it away; I was holding on for dear life. Although I had the safety harness, it did not help my mojo; I still felt impending doom. I took one step at a time, praying not to fall for a number of reasons. Firstly, I did not want to hurt myself; Secondly, I did not want to land on my friends, and lastly I wanted this to be my first and last successful rock climb.

Petros Eshetu

Each step and grip seemed to take hours of toil and sweat. Perspiration ran in a steady stream down my back, arms and fingers. Suddenly, the rock began working with me; it seemed to offer cracks to hold my feet. I did it! I made it to the top, scratched and bruised with my t-shirt drenched in sweat. Finally, I took my first deep breath since climbing the boulder. While exhaling, I realized we had to jump to another boulder.

That rock looked pleasant, with vegetation, a few trees and bright yellow and red flowers. I thought to myself, "I can jump that." But then, I made a mistake; I looked down! Suddenly, the hair on my neck stood up, and my heart pounded as though it were about to leap out of my chest. Fear returned with the "what if" scenario. "What goes up must come down" had not crossed my mind up until that moment.

While I was wiping the sweat away from the previous climb, I prepared mentally for the next challenge. I focused hard on my target and prepared to jump. My heart was pounding; everything fell silent except for the sound of my breathing.

I took a deep breath, and jumped. As I became airborne, I felt an unfamiliar sense of freedom. At that moment, all fear and doubt disappeared. Once I focused on the leap, it was as though I was floating on air. "Wow, I made it," I thought. "I'm on the

I came. I saw. I jumped!

other side." As though I had won an Olympic race, I swung both arms in the air as a sign of triumph.

I learned two important lessons from that jump all those years ago: First, focus on the moment, Secondly, to be present in my life. Looking beyond doubt and fear, once I jumped, none of it mattered. It did not matter how I landed, whether I fell on my hands and knees, or on my shoulder, or flat on my face. It was all about the jump.

In life, you may reach a point where you need to exit a situation such as:

- The job you hate.
- The relationship that is not working.
- The business that is failing.

Fear and uncertainty can hold us back from making necessary changes. This book is all about taking that leap of faith. Throughout this book, I refer to this principle as "jumping."

Life: When you zig, it zags.

Throughout my career, I've had jobs where I stayed too long and should have jumped earlier. I had a sales job that was so stressful I became ill. The long, agonizing hours made me want to smash my head through the computer screen in front of me. My office surroundings were tense with all of the personality conflicts and endless competition among my colleagues.

Workdays had become silent and stressful. I was exhausted; I was becoming someone I would not want to have as a friend - that negative person who had slowly lost the energy to make himself feel alive; I knew something had to change. I had become the guy who no longer wanted to explore new things.

That is not me. I am, by nature, an adventurous person. In fact, it seems that my interests, devotions, and desires are constantly changing and evolving.

So, after a year in the workforce, I went back to school for my MBA, thinking that an advanced degree would help me to land a better job. I felt my life needed a change, and I worried that I was not living up to my potential. I was not meeting the expectations of others. Even four years after achieving my MBA, I still was not sure that I was in the right profession. On the weekends, I needed a whole day to recover from feeling burnt out and tired. I was not sure if I was content or simply miserable. It felt as though I needed permission:

- to quit my job without feeling like a quitter;
- to put me first without feeling selfish;

I came. I saw. I jumped!

- to not care about what others thought without feeling judged;
- to take risks and to make mistakes without feeling like a failure.

It is a strange place to be when you have a job you hate and yet at the same time pray you do not get fired. I needed to live my life on my terms without being apologetic about it.

Reaching a crossroads

I worked with wonderful people; I was well-paid, and I had challenging work; nonetheless, I always felt a yearning for something more rewarding and meaningful. I knew it was not money or success that I wanted; it was fulfillment.

Often, you hear the gentle whisper of your inner voice nudging you toward a new path. This inner voice speaks the true yearnings of your heart. If you ignore it, you eventually land at an important crossroad in your life. That is what happened to me.

I had a high paying job that many would want. I had great benefits; I could work from home in a stable company with a great team environment and a laid-back boss. My friends said I was crazy to even think of leaving such a comfortable job. They would say, "you should be grateful for your job. Some people can't even find jobs in this economy." I would nod my head in agreement, and later I would feel guilty for even having those thoughts. So, I placed my ambitions aside and got back to my routine.

I was running frantically like in a hamster wheel. If I tried to get out of that cycle, I felt compelled to rush back in. I did a lot of running, but I always stayed in the same place. I had fallen out of love with my work, and I found myself repeatedly looking at the computer screen and asking, "Why am I doing this?"

My work had no meaning, and I felt no real connection to it. Something was missing. I needed something fresh and different. The signs were all there for a change. My inner voice kept telling me to get out and start afresh. This voice became louder and louder. It reached a point where all I could hear was, "stop wasting time, stop dreaming and start living now!" Seemingly, somewhere along life's journey, I got lost ending up in a desert alone, walking aimlessly without direction.

Some of the issues that hold us back are the beliefs that what we are doing is the only thing we can do and that our skills are not transferable, and that no other path could be as amazing as the one we are already on.

I came. I saw. I jumped!

As you read this book, you will find out that not only are the above statements false, but you can take your current skills and experience into a new direction.

The million-dollar question: What do I want?

"What I want," is easy to ask but difficult to answer. A better question might be, "What do I not want?"

- I do not want to remain stagnant in my growth.
- I do not want to live an ordinary life.
- I do not want to continue the status quo.

If you flip this thinking around:
- I always want to grow.
- I want to live an extraordinary life.
- I want to live a meaningful life helping others.

Making a U-turn

The time finally arrived in my life where I decided to jump out of the rat race. I came, I saw, and I jumped.

Petros Eshetu

I made it my mission to find my life's passion and purpose. I spent months and hundreds of hours researching various topics. I spent tens of thousands of dollars hiring coaches to help me gain clarity during my period of self-discovery. I even went so far as paying successful entrepreneurs for their wisdom.

After a year of reflection, research, and gaining insights from different people, I eventually found my answers. The result was not what I expected, and my life has since taken a full turn. My vision is no longer blurry, and my dreams have grown bigger than I ever imagined. I have made more progress in the last five months than I made in the previous five years. I have learned the same lessons and strategies others have used to discover their passions. I have applied these lessons to my life with phenomenal results, so I am sharing them in this book.

Today, I love my life, and I wake up every day with a purpose. This awakening began when I decided to make the jump into a life I wanted.

Before you jump, you need to know what it is that you want, and you must be certain that you are headed towards your dream and not toward someone else's idea of your dream.

You could climb a mountain and reach the top only to find you climbed the wrong mountain. Maybe your parents or

I came. I saw. I jumped!

teachers wanted you to be an engineer, a doctor or a lawyer, but deep down, you always wanted to have a different career, maybe a chef, a pilot, a photographer or a painter. There is no right or wrong profession, just as long as that the profession aligns with who you are.

The distance to the top

A mountain has different altitudes. There is a bottom section, a middle and a peak. To reach the top, you must go up, but the path will not always be direct. At any point, you might need to descend or change directions. There is no staircase or straight path to the top. You may have to cross a stream, jump over a boulder or experience extreme temperatures. You will have doubts and fears especially when you become exhausted and frozen during your climb. You may feel you cannot continue because the journey is too difficult. You must fight urges to return to your comfortable life and comfortable job. During these moments your epiphany may arrive, and your strength will be renewed to keep going forward.

"Life is a journey, not a destination"-Ralph Waldo Emerson

Each of us is climbing a mountain in our lives. Pursuing that big goal.Some of us are climbing one that was chosen by us.

Petros Eshetu

Some of us are climbing one that was chosen for us.

So, tell me:

- Whose mountain are you climbing right now?
- Is this the mountain you want to be climbing?
- Have you taken the time to know, deep within, which mountain you are meant to climb?

Find that mountain; one that has meaning to you; and jump to it! What legacy are you going to leave on this earth? Would you want to be remembered for climbing a small hill or climbing Mt. Everest?

I came. I saw. I jumped!

Promises

1. The main goal of this book is to help you gain clarity in your life, and discover your true passion and purpose. Clarity about what you want gives you momentum for action.

2. I will share stories from my journey, both challenges, and successes. More importantly, I will show you how I succeeded in finding the work I love; the work that gives me the fulfillment and happiness I have always sought. I will also include stories of other people's triumphs.

3. You will learn strategies for making your own jump. It does not always mean that you should quit your job immediately; perhaps you should take mini-jumps. Your strategy could involve experimenting with different passions before making the final jump, so you can maintain your lifestyle while you discover what activities you love.

4. Warning: this book is not designed for people who want a quick fix for their life or career challenges. Each of us has a unique career path, so this book presents multiple strategies

that are not a one-size-fits-all solution. The results you attain depends on the effort you make.

5. By the time you finish reading this book, you will learn more about your passion or purpose. Discovering a passion or a purpose is a process. If you are one of the lucky people who rapidly discovers answers, then I am glad to have simply assisted you in that process. Now, if it takes a week, a month, or a year, I have absolute faith that the answers will reveal itself to you with perfect timing. The point of this book is to help you with the process of individual self-discovery.

6. I promise that this book will help you decide whether you are headed in the right direction toward your passion, or whether you're moving further away from your calling or purpose. I suggest that you study this book as a reference for self-reflection on your journey.

7. Even if you already know your purpose and your passion, this book will help you arrive there more rapidly. If you are already living a purpose-filled life and doing what you love, reading this book will give you tools for deeper clarity and for refreshing your goals and visions as you move forward with greater confidence.

I wish you the best of luck, and I am honored to be on this

I came. I saw. I jumped!

journey with you.

Begin Now

"The scariest moment is always just before you start" - Stephen King

Now is the time to get out of your cubicle and corporate crossfire and to focus on your vision; turn those eight empty hours a day into excitement and energy! You do not have to climb someone else's mountain. You can reach the peak of who you truly are. It's doable so let's start today.

By reading this far, you have already made a small jump toward your goals. This book has the tools and directions for your ascent. Now let's get to climbing.

Petros Eshetu

I came. I saw. I jumped!

Chapter 1

Life is too short to be a corporate slave

"No one is truly free; they are a slave to wealth, fortune, the law, or other people restraining them from acting according to their will."

- Euripides

My red wrists scarred by ropes, I was a slave to a master I call a Corporate Prison. When I crawled to the top of the heap, I jumped and landed in a pile of confusion with my new corporate life. "Now what," I thought? I never dreamed I'd be asking myself this question after working hard, getting my education, and sailing off to the corporate world to begin my career. I thought I had finally made it, and I believed that everything would work out, I found myself in an environment where abilities were constrained and success defined by a corporate culture.

As time went on, I came to realize I was part of a system. A system that defined success by salary, by promotion record, and by quarterly progress. A system where growth was defined by how well you clawed your way to the top of the corporate ladder. This system was not freedom. This system was stepping into a cell.

A serial job hopper

Struggling to break free, I became a "serial job hopper." Nothing seemed to satisfy me. I found most positions boring or unchallenging; I became obsessed with external factors like bad co-workers, unpleasant work environments, terrible work cultures, and low wages to validate my job hopping.

Then I found what I thought was my dream job. The kind of job that did not come with all of the issues associated with my past positions. My new job offered great pay and benefits, a stellar boss, good work-life balance, a team mentality, challenging work, open work culture and company stability; I couldn't believe it! Convinced it was paradise, I felt I could not ask for more.

At this point, I was comfortable with my life; I thought that this employment was as close to freedom as I could get. Eventually, the excitement and glitter faded, and I found myself steadily sinking into the familiar feelings of discontent, boredom, and misery.

I came. I saw. I jumped!

"How can this be," I asked myself. "Why am I feeling this way?" "Isn't this position exactly what I wanted?" I wondered if I was just ungrateful or unappreciative. Deep down, I knew there was something more, but I could not put my finger on it.

It soon occurred to me that the job was not fulfilling. I went to work, and eight hours later, I left feeling depleted. I found myself stuck in a rut, and before I knew it, two years had passed. Where did those two years go? Had I been in a trance?

My spirit was dead because I felt as though I had been sucked into a vacuum of eight empty hours for months, and those months had become years, and those years were gone,

"Is this it?" I asked myself.

I had worked so hard to get to where I was. I could not understand why I was so miserable. I could no longer blame that annoying, dragon-breath co-worker whose toxic fire-breath killed any words that left his mouth. Nor could I blame the micro-managing boss. Something was missing, I thought, something important. I decided to take a long, hard look in the mirror; the answer became stunningly clear. It's me!

Petros Eshetu

Emancipation and the straw that broke the camel's back

One day, a new opportunity presented itself. I'd had my eye on this company for a long time. I had applied earlier with them in my career, but I never got a response. Now I was being offered the chance to interview there for a financial position. I was excited by the prospect of moving to this company; I envisioned what I might accomplish there and what promise this cool, new environment and culture offered me: a light to brighten my darkness and bring relief for my misery.

Now, keep in mind that I had gone through this same cycle in the last three job applications. I have no idea why I thought this would be different. Still, I rode the wave of hope and excitement, if only for a few hours, to escape the boredom of my current job.

On the day of the interview, I felt confident. The recruiter called, and we talked for about thirty minutes. It went well, or so I thought. Two days later I received the email rejection.

Since I had interviewed for many jobs before, I felt somewhat immune to rejection, or at the least, I didn't let it deter my drive and determination to succeed. I might be bummed out for an hour or so,

I came. I saw. I jumped!

but I would go on with my day, and not look back so I can chase a new opportunity. However, I expected this rejection to cut deeper. Not only did I want to work for this company, but I was also desperate to exit my current, miserable position. This time was different! I was not disappointed, sad, or hurt. I felt a sense of relief.

"Wait, relief," I thought? "Why do I feel relief? Where's my disappointment? Why am I not sad or angry?"

I kept telling myself, that I needed to be disappointed and sad. "Come on; you just got rejected by your favorite company. What is wrong with you?"

Suddenly, a smile fell over my face. I felt relaxed and oddly calm. Taking a deep breath, I sighed with relief as though a huge weight had been lifted off of my shoulders. Although I was confused and perplexed in the days that followed the rejection, this was the first distinct sign that something had to change. What I was thinking was different than what I was feeling; a battle was raging between my mind and my heart. What I realized was that a career in finance was no longer fulfilling. I am not sure it ever was.

Then, one Friday, while I was working from home, I switched on my laptop and began reading my work emails. Stress began to build and with it came anger and its friend, frustration. The anger was a result of the wasted time and effort I had spent performing work that had no meaning for me. The question of what to do next paralyzed me with worry. Finally, I reached the point; enough is enough. And then, I had an epiphany; "I do not have to do this. Nobody is putting a gun to my head. I do have a choice."

Finally, the turning point arrived. I chose not to accept this hopeless feeling; I decided it was time to write the script of my life rather than allowing others to write it for me.

Who am I? What steps did I take to get here?

My first step on my journey of discovery involved extensive reflection. I asked myself: "How did I end up in finance anyway. Did I choose this direction or was this direction chosen for me?

I looked deep into my memory archives and returned to the time when I first thought of pursuing a career in finance. I remembered that I had friends in my sophomore year that wanted me to join them in their careers in finance. I was good with numbers, so at the time I thought, "Why not?" I didn't know what I wanted to

I came. I saw. I jumped!

do anyway. Besides, I thought my friends knew what was best for me. They knew my capabilities, and I was always a follower, so I didn't question their suggestions. Now, I realize that following the beliefs of others may lead me where I may not want to go.

My career in finance began as a result of allowing other people, my friends, to decide my destiny. I know now that I have to take control of my life and my choices because no one knows my capabilities as well as I do. I had fallen into someone else's plan because I did not have one of my own.

As I assembled the puzzle of my life, I could not help feeling angry and upset at first, toward those who had persuaded me many years ago and later, towards myself for not knowing who I was, and for not making my own decisions. At that time, I did not have the courage or knowledge to make my own choice.

"If I had just known then what I know now, how different my life would have been," I thought.

This conclusion was a tough pill to swallow. Eventually, I accepted what's done is done. I needed to forgive myself, and let go of what happened in the past. I began to be thankful and grateful for this awakening and having a chance to alter my destiny.

Petros Eshetu

How about you? Have you gotten into a career because you were advised by family or friends only to realize later that it wasn't for you? Well, I'm here to tell you that this happens to many people and it is not your fault. When we are young, most of us are not well-equipped with the experience and decision-making skills we need to decide about important decisions, so we think it is wise to act on the advice of other people we trust. There is no crystal ball or fortune teller to guarantee the results of actions we take.

The next step was to determine what I truly did want; what my true passion was, and what I would love to do. I realized that I needed a plan and a vision for my life, or I would again fall into the same trap, of allowing other people to make my decisions. Questions about what I truly want and what my true passion is, are easy to ask, but much more difficult to answer. I decided to make it my mission to discover my answers, and I'm going to share with you the solutions and tools I discovered along the way.

I came. I saw. I jumped!

The journey

Once I became crystal clear about what I wanted, I made the "jump." As I mentioned earlier, jumping does not have to be quitting your job, at least not right now. However, you do need to devise a clear vision of your future and what you want. Don't worry; I've got you covered, and I will help guide you through the "jump." I'm going to share my experience, the lessons and the strategies that I applied on my journey after I discovered what I love to do, and ultimately, my purpose.

Before my leap of faith, I hesitated to quit my job for many months because of fear of the unknown. I had no plan, so I did not know where to begin. I then asked myself, "If I die tomorrow, will I regret not making this decision to quit my job?" I paused for a couple of seconds. I closed my eyes, and I looked deep within, "Yes, I would have regrets if I did not make this decision." At that moment, I decided to quit my job, and I have not looked back since.

I had no idea what was going to happen next. I had no plan B. But somehow, I got a sense that everything would work out. I was learning to trust and believe in myself. My wife was a great source of support; she gave me her blessing and told me to follow my heart, I finally let go and stopped following the life prescribed to me.

The road on your journey will not always be easy or straightforward. You must zig and zag, and lean with the twists and turns. It took me a while to come to this certainty in my life. Many hours of research, experimenting and meeting people from a variety of backgrounds had to happen first.

On life's regrets

In her book, *The Top Five Regrets of The Dying*, Bonnie Ware, an Australian hospice nurse, recorded her dying patients' regrets. Over the years, Bonnie had many patients who had only a few weeks left to live. It was during those last few weeks of her patient's life that they gained the most insight over the question of whether they had really lived or not. They told her about their pleasant memories and their painful regrets. Do you know what their number one common regret was? "I wish I had the courage to live a life true to myself." They wished that they had followed their own paths and dreams rather than following the dreams of others. These dying patients

I came. I saw. I jumped!

wished that they'd had the courage to design their lives and align their lives with their authentic selves.

I always walk past a nearby cemetery in my neighborhood. Beyond the large fence surrounding the graveyard, one can see beautiful green grass and flowers that are well-maintained by the groundskeepers in the area. There are so many gravestones, both large and small, with different family names. I often wondered how many unfulfilled dreams and inventions are now buried, never to be realized: Inventions that could have changed modern life. Books and stories that were left untold that could have impacted millions of lives.

For example, what if Thomas Edison were never born, or what if fear prevented his pursuit of his dreams? Would we have useful electricity, recorded movies, music, and other inventions? Personally, I do not think so; at the very least, we would not have had them so soon.

My point is that Thomas Edison was an active participant in his life. He pursued his passion for invention that led to technologies that changed the world. The world is a better place because he was born and because he had the courage to chase his dreams. In the

Petros Eshetu

words of Paul Arden, "It's better to regret what you have done than what you have not."

So, I asked myself, "Whose dreams are you living for? Whose mountains are you climbing? Are you following what others wanted you to do or are you following your own path? Is it time to jump to your own dream?"

I came. I saw. I jumped!

The #1 killer of dreams is procrastination.

I learned a lesson about procrastination when a good family friend died in late 2015. Her name was Helaine, and she was like a second mother to me. In her 60's, Helaine was the strongest woman I knew. She lived a life of purpose, always eating healthy and exercising regularly for decades. Her favorite pastime was reading. After all, she was a retired professor. I stayed with her for two years while I was working towards my MBA. Helaine loved to travel around the world visiting and keeping in touch with former students and friends.

As I sat in the synagogue at her funeral in downtown Charleston, South Carolina, I could not help but be amazed by all of her accomplishments as the Rabbi announced them. Helaine was an avid traveler, a professor, but more importantly for me, a good friend. I respected and admired her courage to go after what she wanted without hesitation or apologies. She did everything she wanted to do in her life, and she did it on her terms.

As I sat in the synagogue reflecting on my life, I considered of all the things I still hoped to accomplish. I never realized how fragile life was, and I did not know when my time would come. If I die tomorrow, I wondered, will I die as an analyst or will I die while chasing my dream. This experience made me aware of the brevity of life, and it gave me the urgency to chase my goals and to stop procrastinating.

Embracing the moment and beginning to take even the smallest action towards my dreams was liberating. Nothing can be more empowering and freeing than the realization that life is short. This reality will ignite a fire, and create an urgency to act and pursue goals. However, before you act on your dream, you first need to identify what it is that you want. You must determine your passion and purpose.

"Procrastination is one of the most common and deadliest of diseases, and its toll on success and happiness is heavy." -Wayne Dyer

So, let's take a moment to fill in the blank: Before I die, I want to…

I came. I saw. I jumped!

Petros Eshetu

I came. I saw. I jumped!

Chapter 2

Purpose and passion

In the 1940's, there was a young girl in Cuba named Celia who was a schoolteacher. She loved to sing and had the most amazing voice that stopped people in their tracks when they heard her sing. Everyone, including her mother and friends, recognized that Celia's gift was her voice, and that one day she would become a singer and huge superstar.

Everyone praised Celia for her talents. Everyone, except for the one person Celia respected and admired most, her father. Her father worked on the Cuban Railroad, and did not approve of her singing. He insisted that his daughter remain a teacher and not attempt to sing professionally.

Celia could not chase her dream and fulfill her father's expectations at the same time. She was torn. The clash between Celia's burning desire and her father's restrictions was a source of frustration rather than fulfillment.

That was until one day…

Before I tell you rest of the story, let's address the family culture dynamic that has a huge impact on our career choice.

Family culture- Escaping the established form of government

Many times, you embark on a career that was chosen for you, most likely by your parents or close friends. Maybe there was someone you looked up to, a mentor, who gave you direction to follow.

There are a few people who early in their life knew what they loved to do. A person with that knowledge combined with a great support system has many advantages that most of us do not have. If you're one of these people, that's great! Consider yourself to be rarely fortunate. For the rest of us, the time has come to figure it out. I belonged to the latter group. I know the feeling of not knowing what I'd love to do so to serve others, and make a decent income doing it.

Think back to when you were a child. Did you dream of being a fireman, painter or, perhaps an artist? Somehow as we get older,

I came. I saw. I jumped!

childhood dreams fade with life's demands. People tell you to be realistic and to give up those dreams. Others may urge their beliefs on you to find a stable career, to become a doctor, an engineer, a lawyer or a businessman. Without your knowledge, and when you are young, seeds are planted within your mind. Those seeds grow and blossom into a self-identity which in reality is based on the beliefs of others. All of the planting is done by people with the best intentions. Sometimes mental gardening works out and sometimes it doesn't.

Generational Differences

Parents are from a different era than their children. Associating your passion with a career may not have been a choice at all for your parents. The idea of doing work you love may have been a difficult concept for them and other members of their generation. Parents did what they had to do to pay the bills and more importantly, take care of their family. Stability was valued in all areas of life. I have known this in my life; my dad worked for the same company for over 20 years before retiring. The world we live in now is so different and unpredictable, compared to the world of our parents' time.

Petros Eshetu

Companies that once dominated their industries have now disappeared (or become irrelevant) because of competition and technical innovation. There are many examples like Kodak, a company that once dominated the photography industry, underestimated the future of digital photography and did not see the rise and popularity of camera phones.

Today no company or job is safe or secure. A job that appears to be stable can be eliminated in a moment. Rapid change is a characteristic of our society. You might work four or more jobs before retirement. The internet allows us to find a job anywhere in the world within a second. Now, I can find job opportunities in the United States or anywhere in the world. I can interview using Skype or any other online video conferencing tool.

You may choose a career in law enforcement, the military or business that your family members have followed for generations. In that family environment, subtle expectations of what you should be, have been transmitted so many times that you that you have created your identity and acceptance around it.

This environment reminds me of a TV show, Blue Bloods, about a family involved in law enforcement. One son is a New York Police Department detective and a former Marine. Another son is a

I came. I saw. I jumped!

police officer; the daughter is a district attorney, and her father is the Police Commissioner. The grandfather, a former Police Commissioner, is a retired.

Every Sunday night, the members of the Blue Bloods family sit around the dinner table talking about work. The children are listening and hearing the stories and debates. They question their parent and grandparents about a controversial case or an unfavorable court decision. The children, in a way, are preparing to follow in their parents' footsteps. Even though the Blue Blood series is fiction, it closely resembles a real-world situation, where family influences shape career choices.

Under these influences, it becomes easy for an individual to choose a career based on other peoples' plans and not consider their own.

- What is your family's history?
- Could your family's belief system have influenced you to make an unsatisfactory career choice?

What is my passion?

Its a fair question to ask. I have asked myself this question many times in the last few years. There were days when I was inspired. I would wake up energetic, and willing to tackle new projects. But there were other days when I was lazy, and not excited about life. I had no motivation dragged my feet to accomplish tasks. This yo-yo cycle of energy occurred frequently. Some days were worse than others, and I did not know what was going on. When I saw others around me who were successful I would ask myself, "What do they know that I do not? What am I missing? How is it that I do not yet know what I really want?"

Everywhere I kept hearing "follow your passion." What does that even mean? Don't you need to know what your passion is before you can follow it?

How do I select a passion if I have so many?

The other concern is, what if you have many passions? For me, I love soccer, dancing, reading, art, business and more. How do you know which is the appropriate one to select? How do you find that passion?

I came. I saw. I jumped!

At first, I went about answering this question in the wrong way. Later I realized, passion is not something I can find outside of myself but rather its something that is internal within me. My passion is a journey from within, and not outside of me. Many times, I would ask, "What is my passion? I could not answer. Why? Because passion is connected to how I feel as the result of some activity, and not to what I think. How do you feel when you carry out certain activities? Are you excited, curious or bored? What types of activities do you engage in where time just flies, and you take no notice? Keep in mind passion is a journey and not a destination. So, when you hear, "Follow your passion," that phrase translates into, "Follow your journey."

Which passion should you choose to pursue? All of them! Okay, maybe not all of them, and at least not all at the same time. Experiment with each one. Get a feel for the aspects of a task you like most, or like the least. Eventually, you will have a list of good things that you will seek in your next job. In Chapter 4, we will discuss in greater detail how to try out your passions.

"Passion is the genesis of genius" by Galileo Galilei

3 Step Formula to Fulfillment

The simple formula to obtain fulfillment in your life is:

Gift + Vehicle + Purpose (G+V+P)

A skill you were born with is a gift (G). A vehicle (V) is what you use to transport your gift to your dream life. Purpose (P) is using your gift to serve others.

This section will explain how you can apply this formula in your life.

1. **Follow your gift**   (G) +V+P

Alternatively, instead of a follow your passion notion, why not approach it as follow your gift?

What is your gift? A gift is a special skill that you have. I believe that each one of us was born with a gift. When you use your gift, the activity result you demonstrate is noticeably better than that of other people who are doing the same thing. It's your talent. It is that trait

I came. I saw. I jumped!

that compels other people to compliment you and ask you about it. Maybe you get compliments: "Thanks for organizing the dinner party last week," or "thanks for connecting me to Jane from the Medical device company." Maybe you get questions, "how do I invest money wisely"? Perhaps you are good at coaching, creating art, listening, networking, leading, or advising.

For example, my gifts are reading, listening, and writing. I love reading books, all day every day. Reading evokes different emotions and feelings from within me. Stories energize me. In my apartment, books are everywhere, on the floor, on the shelves, and in the cupboard. People tell me when they visit that they feel like they are entering a library. Of course, I take that as a compliment.

Knowing your gift

There are several ways you can identify your gift. Ask yourself, "What do I love to teach? What activities or topics of conversation excites me? If I won a billion dollars in the lottery, what would I do every day?

Here are some other questions to get your creative juices flowing.

- What are the three types of magazines you might buy at a store?

- What website, other than social media, do you like to visit?

- When you were seven years old, what did you want to be?

- What would you do if you knew you could not fail?

- What do you love to do in your spare time?

You can also ask close friends and family about your talents. These people can tell you quickly, and their answers might surprise you.

When I asked friends and family what my strengths were, many replied that I was a good listener and that I helped them get clear about their next steps in making decisions. I remembered that some of my friends, would call me to talk about their concerns or needed advice, and I was happy to listen. At the end of our conversation, they would always feel better and more confident about what they needed to do next.

Questions to ask family and relatives include

- What was I good at as a child?

- What excited me when I was a child? What would make me angry or upset?

- What did I spend most of my time doing?

I came. I saw. I jumped!

- Do you remember a time, or have a story about noticing a talent in me?

- What did I say about what I would want to do when I grew up?

Before asking these questions, I suggest that you tell them that you will not get defensive or upset when they answer. Remember, you want their honest feedback, even if you do not agree with it, or do not see yourself in that light.

You can tell family and friends that these questions are for part of a course you are taking to help you consider your next career or job. This explanation will reduce their apprehension, so they are more likely to tell you what you need to hear rather than what they think you want to hear.

I recommend that you ask three or more close family or friends so you can discover the common themes among their answers.

Questions to ask friends, coworkers, boss, etc. include

- What would you say my strengths and gifts are?
- How would you describe me to someone else?

- Do you remember an incident where I did something that surprised and delighted you?

- How do I respond to challenges or conflicts?

- When have I been happiest in my life?

If you can afford it, I would also recommend working with a career or a life coach, to help you define the next steps. A coach can give you feedback, and help you work through stumbling blocks that you may encounter. A coach can be your accountability person, and help you expand your limits.

Another way to figure out what you aspire to be is to examine the lives of prominent people that you admire. For example, I look up to Wayne Dyer, Tony Robbins, Brian Tracy, T. Harv Ecker, Simon Sinek and other personal development figures. There was something about them that I wanted to incorporate into my life. I learned as much as I could about them because I saw these investigations as opportunities to learn more about myself and to dig deeper into identifying my talents.

So, take a minute to write down the names of people you admire most. Who inspires you? What traits or skills do they have

I came. I saw. I jumped!

that you admire? Perhaps you relate to them in some way that connects to what you want in your life or career.

Take an online Personality Test *(optional)*

There are numerous online personality tests that can help you on your strength assesment. The three most popular online sites for these tests that I have used are:

- 16 Personalities

  www.16personalities.com

- Gallup strength finder

  www.gallupstrengthscenter.com

- Myer & Briggs Test

  www.myersbriggs.org

If you are working, check to see if your employer offers free, in-depth analysis for employees. If you're a student, see if your school offers free personality tests at the above mentioned online sites.

Personality assessments can provide insights into your talents, working style, and values. You can use these assessments as tools to guide you in addition to the other recommendations I have made.

Oops, wrong turn

My path to self-discovery was not straightforward. I took a lot of twists and turns, and I made a lot of mistakes. I spent money on courses and classes I should never have taken. Many times, I had to stop, take a step back, and reassess. Sometimes I had to go back to the drawing board. You might take the two steps forward and one step back approach. Remember, failure is part of the process. Embrace the valuable lessons that come from it.

I remember one of my biggest mistakes on my journey was signing up for a two thousand- dollar course that I realized later I did not need. The money was not refundable. I was already stressed because I did not have an income at the time. After that experience, I was careful about any courses .I learned to be more clear and certain that the results would justify the investment.

Follow the yellow brick road

I came. I saw. I jumped!

Since I had helped friends and family with job advice, I figured I would be a career coach; I liked doing it. Writing resumes and cover letters was easy for me. I talked to a few career coaches to get insight into this career. I already had my career coach, Lindsey, whom I worked with during my career change. I had a conversation with Lindsey which reinforced what I wanted to do.

Me: "I'm still not sure on my final career path."

Lindsey: "What do you mean?"

Me: "I like career coaching, but something is missing, or not fully clicking."

Lindsey: "Do you feel like you're not going in the right direction?"

Me: "It's not that; I'm heading in the right direction. It just I don't know if career coaching is the destination. I like the coaching part, though."

Lindsey: "Alright! Let me ask you. What type of books or magazines do you like read often?"

Me: "Hmmm, mostly I like to read personal development or self-help type of books or magazines. I enjoy learning different ways I can improve on myself."

I paused, realizing something special at that moment; a light bulb came on in my head!

Me: "Of course, that's it! It's been staring at my face the whole time. How can I not see it? I'm meant to be a Personal Development Coach.

I'm always reading about the subjects and applying different ideas in my life, and have seen massive improvements. Most people I admire are all from the self-improvement category, and are helping to transform people's lives."

I wasn't sure about Lindsey's intent when she asked that question, but I just ran with it. I was over the moon with this realization. I enjoyed helping people find their strengths, and I loved to work on their personal growth.

2. Choose the right vehicle $\quad$ G + (V) + P

Knowing the right vehicle to transform your gift into your dream life is important. The right vehicle is that specific area of interest that triggers your curiosity, and a desire to learn more about its latest developments.

Maybe you enjoy reading about the newest technological innovation, in cars, or trends in fashion or travel. Ask yourself, "Is there an industry I want to learn more about?"

It is important to make sure that your job hones your gift. All industries have wide ranges of jobs for you to consider.

I came. I saw. I jumped!

I will use the finance industry as an example because I know it well. You could be a:

- Financial analyst (if you are analytically-gifted)
- Financial coach (if you are listening-gifted person)
- Financial sales professional (for persuasion-gifted person)

I am over-generalizing, and I know you may have multiple skills for different job segments. However, my point is that some roles require stronger skills that play to your strengths.

A great example of a person who changed vehicles in his career is the comedian Steve Harvey. Steve Harvey's career started off as a stand-up comedian; he then hosted live shows at Showtime at the Apollo. He had a television show, The Steve Harvey Show. Movies came next; then a radio show. He became a bestselling author; he hosted a daytime television show as well as a game show, Family Feud.

Steve's gift, is his humor, making people laugh. However, the vehicle (medium) in which he applied his gift changed over time. As he became more successful, he learned new and complementary skills for his gift that opened doors and offered new opportunities. Steve Harvey is not just a comedian anymore; he has become an entrepreneur, a television host, a producer, a radio personality, an actor, and an author.

Tony Robbins, the most well-known motivational speaker in the world, is another person who learned complementary skills. His core skill is speaking. His gift is commanding the stage and grabbing people's attention when he speaks. Robbin's mission in life is to help and inspire as many people as he can to transform their lives. He knew that to fulfill his mission and make a large impact on the world; he would need to learn some business skills.

Now, decades later, Tony runs billion-dollar companies. If you had asked him at the beginning of his career if he wanted to become an entrepreneur or businessman, he probably would have told you no. However, on his way toward fulfilling his mission, he leveraged his complementary skills. Tony changed the vehicle when the opportunity appeared.

As you progress in your career, you may also need to re-invent yourself. Sometimes, that may mean changing vehicles and being open to new opportunities that require learning a new skill.

My gift is listening, reading, and sharing my knowledge through writing. I could have spread my message using different vehicles (methods). I could have chosen to be a teacher, a speaker, a coach, or a consultant. I could have chosen to create an online course,

I came. I saw. I jumped!

create a video, write a book, start a podcast or be a journalist. Personally, I enjoy writing and coaching. It comes easily, and I'm always eager to learn new ways to teach.

You may prefer sharing your knowledge or expertise through YouTube videos. You may feel more comfortable expressing yourself with a video format rather than written one. Perhaps you can do both. Find that vehicle that feels authentic to you. Do not focus on what others are doing.

Change vehicles with passion

As you grow and mature, so does your passion. As you settle into one passion, you might learn and absorb so much in a field that you feel that you want to try something different. Maybe the vehicle you used just ran out of fuel, or the engine broke down. At times, you may need to change vehicles to arrive at your destination.

I believe that knowing your gift and using it is the key to fulfillment. However, you need to determine if the vehicle is right for you. You should consistently question whether or not your current vehicle excites you, or is helping add value to others.

Petros Eshetu

"Finding the right vehicle for your gift will be the key to moving your gift from a dream to a reality" - Steve Harvey

- Make a list the best vehicles for your gift today.
- Write down the kind of vehicles that you would like to use for your gifts 5 to 10 years from now.

3. Know your purpose? G + V + ⓟ

I believe that we are all born with a purpose. Some people may know their purpose, while others are still searching for it.

What lights you up? What activities energize you? What activities drain your energy?

These are important questions. The energy at the core of who you are is displayed when you work on your life's purpose. When thinking about your purpose, do not look at it as changing who you are, but rather as being a better version of who you are.

Your purpose connects to work that gives you an energetic drive. This work or activity is easy for you because you love it, even though you have spent hundreds of hours and effort on it. The activity may be difficult in the eyes of other people, but you enjoy the

I came. I saw. I jumped!

activity because you are flowing with the energy when you are doing it.

For example, I mentioned earlier that I love reading and writing. When I'm reading books, I get a thrill, and I am full of energy and excitement, even with just the anticipation that I will learn something new or develop a new insight. I can say that I am addicted to learning.

To help you align with your energy source. I recommend that you make a list of activities that give you energy. List also those activities that diminish your energy. If you are aware of these activities; you will be surprised at what you find.

J.K Rowling, one of the most famous authors in history with her Harry Potter book series is a great example of someone who followed her path and purpose. Her story is a typical rags to riches story. When J.K Rowling started, she was a writer living in a small, one-bedroom apartment without much money. She was not a confident person and unsure of herself most of the time. The only thing that she was 100% sure of, without a single doubt was that she loved writing children's books.

Now the odds of having success in the children's' book category are small. This category is so competitive that many authors do not succeed. Twelve publishers initially rejected her book, until finally, one publisher gave her a chance. The rest is history. The Harry Potter books turned out to be among the fastest-selling books in history.

J.K Rowling knew her purpose was to be a writer. She had a plan and stuck to it despite initial rejections. As a result, she is a massive success. This anecdote is an example of the power you have when you know your purpose. You become well-equipped to persevere through all of your challenges.

Passion vs Purpose

You may be asking, what is the difference between passion and purpose? We know passion is related to your gift. Purpose has more to do with what brought you to this earth. It's the "why you were born." Purpose includes serving others by using your gift and being an active participant in the world. It's the thing that makes you get up in the morning to do what you do. For example, I do not get up every day so I can be a good listener or writer. I wake up with a mindset to serve others and to help transform their lives. My mission is to help people reach their full potential, one dream at a time.

I came. I saw. I jumped!

Passion is that energetic emotion that fuels your dream. Purpose is the drive behind it all.

You must love what you do to be truly successful and fulfilled. To have a fulfilling life, make sure to include giving back to others because giving back empowers your gift to be truly impactful.

Everyone has a gift as part of their individuality. You might not always recognize it, but you do have it. Your gift is connected to your passion. This passion is your energy source. Your purpose will come along once you know your strengths. Choose an appropriate vehicle that aligns with your gift, and fosters the growth of your gift, and includes the addition of complementary skills. Let the flow of your energy guide you in reaching your full potential.

You are a unique individual, and you have a gift that you must share with the world. Before you can hone in on your gift, you need first to identify it. Only then, can you begin to refine and master it. Remember, follow your path, but above all stay true to your authentic self. Follow your path, not somebody else's idea of what your path should be. Only take direction if you are lost, and have no idea of where to go. Other than that, just stay in your lane.

Remember that Cuban girl, Celia the singer I mentioned at the beginning of chapter ? She won first place in a singing contest in Cuba. For Celia winning the prize was not as important as catching the attention of well-known record producers. Later she met with her childhood idol from a popular Cuban singing group who praised and complimented her for her singing voice.

In Celia's mind, the compliment she received from her idol was a sign from the universe that her passion was singing. At that moment, she promised herself that she would pursue her dream regardless of what anyone, including her father, told her. Eventually, Celia replaced her idol in the popular Cuban singing group to become the most well-known and successful Cuban singer of all time. So, who is this Cuban singer I keep talking about? It is none other than Celia Cruz.

Celia not only got her wish to be a famous singer, but she also became a global superstar. She died in 2006, but was by then the most popular Latin artist of the twentieth century, and was renowned as the "Queen of Salsa." She won several Grammy awards and even received a National Medal of Arts award from President Bill Clinton in the 1990's.

I came. I saw. I jumped!

"The two most important days in your life are the day you are born and the day you find out why" - MarkTwain

Petros Eshetu

I came. I saw. I jumped!

Petros Eshetu

Chapter 3

The truth about tasting courage

Standing on the edge of the cliff, I was nervous, sweaty, and just exhausted thinking of what I was about to do. I glanced twice behind me as if to say goodbye to my old world. I felt the cool breeze pass across my face. My legs shook uncontrollably like they would buckle underneath me. The fear of the unknown was all-consuming.

As I peered into the distance, I saw the boulder. It mockingly dared me to jump. I told myself, "Do not look down!" Fear gripped my chest. It was now or never. Somehow, I knew it was the right moment. I glanced back one last time. Assuming a runner's stance, legs slightly apart, I brushed the ground like a bull about to charge. Taking in one last deep breath, I closed my eyes and jumped.

I came. I saw. I jumped!

Knowing when to jump?

The short answer is now! The better question is how big or how far do you want to jump? My intuition told me something I had to change. I knew it was the right time for me to quit my job.

When my lifeless corporate life was over, I reflected positively on my experience. I remain appreciative of the skills I acquired, and for the opportunity to work alongside some amazing people. I became adept at recognizing my weaknesses and improving my strengths. Corporate life also afforded me paid vacations and a distinguished lifestyle.

I realize the values I gained from my corporate job, and I have come to understand that it was directly responsible for setting me on to my true path. I knew I did not want to do this corporate financial work anymore. I needed to re-evaluate my journey. I'm grateful for all the lessons I learned, both good and bad.

According to recent Gallup studies, 70% of the U.S workforce are not mentally engaged in their work. These workers do not love their jobs; many workers go to work dreaming of something more. If this description fits you, take charge of your life and make a change. By finding interest in this book, you are demonstrating a curiosity about finding more fulfillment in your life. Do not settle for a mediocre existence! Connect to your inner strength and energy. You are the only one who can decide what you want out of life.

You must redefine yourself. What does success mean to you? Do you define success by how much money you make or your job title? Is success defined by the size of your house or what type of car you drive? Maybe success is how many followers you have on Instagram? None of these is right or wrong as long as you know what motivates you. I began to define success by how happy I am.

Who am I, if not me?

I used to let the job define me. I'm Petros, a financial analyst. My daily appearance included a starched white shirt and a pen in my right pocket. I smiled at work, but I wasn't overly engaging. Calculations filled my thoughts. Walking around the office, I felt empty inside and disconnected with my surroundings.

Everything became routine. I began each day addressing countless emails in my inbox. Some messages had teasing subject lines like "Urgent" or "ASAP" to coax me to drop everything and focus on their meaningless task.

I came. I saw. I jumped!

I never enjoyed wearing suits to work. I wore my daily business attire as a suit of armor; poised for battle at a moment's notice. Who would I be fighting today? Microsoft? Excel?

Engulfed in loneliness, I remember sitting in the office one day and watching the daily scene. My colleagues were walking around laughing, gossiping, talking about last night's game and so on. It was as if everyone was engaged in witty banter and strategizing ways to reach the top of the corporate ladder. I felt disconnected from their goals because I realized they were no longer my goals.

Honestly, my career aspirations never included managing the office, and I wasn't passionate about that job. I do not mean to cast a negative light on corporate life; it just wasn't for me. I did not utilize my gift effectively, and I needed to change vehicles. I know many people who flourish in corporate settings, and love having a routine, a set schedule, a steady paycheck, and a few vacation days a year. If this is you, great! Just know which side of the fence you are on.

Whenever I thought about quitting, I asked myself:

"How will people treat me if I quit? Will I be an outcast? "

"Will I be viewed differently?"

"If I do not have that job then, where do I belong?"

Overall, I saw myself as a success. Does my status change if I leave the office permanently? The more I thought about these questions, the more nervous, anxious and afraid I became to jump.

I began to realize changing my career meant changing my identity and changing how I viewed myself. Who am I, if not me? Who am I, if I'm not Petros, the financial analyst? In the next chapter, we will delve deeper into the identity change that takes place during a career transition.

D-day; quitting

During the days before and after quitting my job, my emotions rose and fell like a roller coaster ride. After all, this was not a job I hated. This type of work just was not for me. I had good memories of the office managers and my co-workers. I belonged to a great company with competitive benefits and a good salary. From an extrinsic value standpoint, the job was remarkable. I was appreciative and grateful to be there with my team, but I was not happy with my role and my daily tasks. Although I was ready to make a change in my life, I still had mixed emotions about quitting.

I came. I saw. I jumped!

Perhaps you are in the opposite scenario, where you strongly dislike your job or company, and you would gladly quit. Sometimes I would wish my job was one where I despised my boss or co-workers and where quitting would be easy. Fortunately, or unfortunately, depending on how you look at it, that was not my situation. Making the decision to quit my job was a difficult, but integral step in setting myself on the path moving forward.

The night before I quit my job was sleepless. My thoughts were scattered, my brain repeatedly went over each scenario. "Do I stay or do I jump?" I asked myself. I tried to calm my nerves and think positively. I watched television; I listened to relaxing music, and I tried reading a book. Nothing worked. Eventually, I passed out at 3 a.m. sleeping in the same clothes I wore the day before.

Waking up four hours later with sunlight sneaking past the bedroom blinds, I felt afraid and apprehensive. I decided to skip breakfast, so I left my English muffin on the table. I could not tell if the butterflies in my stomach stemmed from the excitement of quitting and starting a new chapter in my life, or if the butterflies were a signal that my body was about to shut down, and I was about to vomit all over the kitchen floor.

Petros Eshetu

Finally, after an hour, I built up the courage to grab my laptop, and write my resignation letter. Mixed emotions flooded my mind as I typed the letter. I was distressed at the thought of not seeing my co-workers again, and I felt guilty for leaving a gap in the team. I was concerned over how my boss and team members would react. Inwardly, I felt pangs of anxiety as I realized I had no Plan B. Despite these feelings, I found myself excited and empowered to control my own destiny.

Underneath it all, I believed it was the right time to leave. I finished writing my resignation email; reviewed the draft, and decided that I was satisfied with the final product. My cursor hovered over the send button for a few minutes. I kept thinking, "Do you really want to do this? Do you know what you're about to do?" Pressing send was final; everything would change; I could not go back.

My heart was pounding like a drum. And then I did it, I jumped. I hit send! The nightmare was over. It was officially the beginning of a new journey in my life. In the days following my resignation, I was both ecstatic and terrified at the same time. I had the freedom to do what I wanted. I was excited. Then the panic set in. At first, I thought, "Yes, I quit my job." Then it changed to, "Oh no, I

I came. I saw. I jumped!

quit my job!" I questioned my motives and my own decision-making process. What was I thinking? What am I going to do now?

Self-doubt consumed me. Although I had doubts before making the jump, I assumed these doubts would subside, and be replaced with self-motivating excitement as I approached this new frontier. I was completely wrong. In fact, my anxiety and doubt quadrupled because I feared the road ahead.

No schedule; what to do today?

With no one telling me to start at eight o'clock, or to take a lunch break; without having a schedule, or having to ask permission to leave, I thought I would have plenty of time to work on side projects. I was wrong. I was less productive than before I quit because I had no sense of urgency to complete my tasks. My focus and energy were well below the level I had when I was working, and I had less spare time. After I had resigned, I needed to develop a schedule, to create "artificial" deadlines, and to also designate time for fun. I set up my daily schedule as follows:

6 a.m. - wake up.

6 a.m. - 8 a.m. - write my book.

Petros Eshetu

8 a.m. - 9 a.m. - eat breakfast.

9 a.m. -11 a.m. - catch up on emails and work on my blog content.

11 p.m. -12 p.m. – workout.

12 p.m. – 2 p.m. - eat lunch.

2 p.m. - 6 p.m. - write my book and online blog.

6 p.m. - 7 p.m. – eat dinner.

7 p.m. - 9 p.m. – write my book.

9 p.m. - midnight – relax, have fun; watch a television show or movie.

This schedule helped me improve my time management by creating artificial time limits for my never-ending work mindset.

Has something similar ever happened to you, where you had never-ending work? Where you had to define a time to call it a day?

Bringing unfinished work home from the office is a habit that's hard to change. Maybe you are trying to meet a work deadline, or you just want to impress your boss. I can relate to those motives because my full-time job was in a fast-paced environment with tight deadlines. So I always had to work extra hours just to keep up. This atmosphere is stressful and takes time away from family or other non-work activities. If you work in a time-sensitive environment, set

I came. I saw. I jumped!

up a time-management schedule so that you can have time for activities that are not work-related.

Designate a time to stop working and to begin focusing on fun activities. See a movie in the middle of the week or visit a nearby zoo. Do anything that takes you out of your normal routine. For many of us just because you have finished work doesn't mean that your mind automatically switches to relaxation mode. Your brain still has thoughts left over from the day. Doing something different will help pull you out of that state.

Tempted by a 30% salary increase

I reached out to switch off my alarm clock only to realize that the phone was ringing. "Another recruiter," I thought. I picked up the phone and heard that polished voice on the other end of the line. The verbal handshake, saying, "We see the skills you developed the last few years and heard that you're a free agent at this point. You have a great resume and experience. We would love to have an interview and offer you a thirty percent salary increase from what you were making at your old firm."

Petros Eshetu

'Tempting offer," I thought. I tried to swallow a dry ball in my throat. The offer sounded good. As I looked at my resume on the table, I noticed a mistake that needed to be corrected. Then I looked towards the kitchen, and I realized that I did not do last night's dishes.

I snapped out and came back to the conversation at hand. I politely let the recruiter know that I appreciated them reaching out to me and that I would keep their name and contact information.

As I hung up the phone, a sense of freedom poured over me. The power of saying no to a tempting offer was liberating. To know that I had a choice about my destiny was wonderful. I could see the old me jumping on that job opportunity in a heartbeat. I reflected on how far I had come from the times when I let the external world control my destiny; now I was taking full control of my future. I am the captain of my own ship. I choose the direction I sail.

When you quit your field of expertise, you are going to still have recruiters and old contacts from your former world reach out to you. It is so tempting, and at the same time humbling, to realize that you are still wanted in the field of expertise that you developed over the years. I learned that to overcome failure is a challenge, but it is just as important is to overcome temptations that can shake you off of

I came. I saw. I jumped!

your path. It's as though you're driving on the road when you see a bright shiny object on the ground. You are tempted to stop your car and pick it up rather than continuing on your journey.

Quitter myth

"Winners never quit; quitters never win." -Vince Lombardi

You might think that if you quit your job you're a failure and you will carry shame with you when you encounter your peers, friends, and family. You are afraid you will be viewed as a quitter.

What I think Vince Lombardi expressed in this quote above is; "you should not abandon your dreams or goals because you have challenges along the way." There are many paths you can take in reaching your goals. For example, a failure in your first business does not mean that you should let go of your dream of being a multi-millionaire or a successful entrepreneur. It just means you will need to try a different business idea to get there.

Paths may change, but your destination will remain the same

I once heard that smart people know when to quit. After all, how can you start a new chapter in your life if you haven't closed the old one yet? As they say, when one door closes, and another one opens.

For me quitting my job to go for what I love to do was initially both heaven and hell all at the same time. If you ask me today, if I regret leaving my job? I would tell you no. It was the right time. You can call it a gut feeling, intuition or just the universe sending me a message to leave. To jump is more of a mental game than a physical one. Is it time for you to face your fears?

- Is it time for you to quit that job you hate?
- Is it time for you to quit that toxic relationship you've been in for years?
- Is it time for you to quit that unprofitable business?

I came. I saw. I jumped!

Petros Eshetu

Chapter 4

Hand and Foot placement- You do not want to fall to your death- the ABC plan

"It's not the mountain we conquer but ourselves" by Edmund Hillary

Jumping without parachute

I did not have an exit strategy when I made my jump. Of course, it's never wise to go into anything new in your life without a plan, especially when it affects your income. It can be a recipe for disaster. There are many people without jobs, and here I am voluntarily leaving a good-paying position. I'm either crazy, or I have a backup job lined up. I would lean more to the former. Culturally, we are taught to have a plan for any life goal one hopes to achieve such as:

I came. I saw. I jumped!

- You want to lose weight: Weight Loss Plan.
- You want to save or invest money: Financial Plan.
- You want to go on vacation: Travel Itinerary.

Planning needs to be part of your life so you can reduce any risk that can potentially hurt you, either financially or emotionally. I know this because I am a planner at heart.

During my whole life, I have been a goal-setting enthusiast to the core. I love planning, and I have always been naturally analytical (attention to detail). For example, whenever I go on any vacation with my wife, Lisa, I plan the trip in detail by:

- Searching for air ticket deals, and playing with different scenarios such as changing dates or routes to get airfare rates.
- Planning daily itineraries.
- Organizing transportation to get to our destinations.

I spend hours and days organizing our trips, and I enjoy every minute of it. I make sure no stones are left unturned. I try to reduce every possible risk so that we have a successful trip. Lisa is more laid back, a go-with-the-flow kind of person when it comes to planning. I now understand why they say opposites attract.

Petros Eshetu

It is very uncharacteristic of me not to have a plan. Nonetheless, I still had the conviction to quit my job with no plan B. In the past, I would have had a backup plan before I quit any job, but again I would only end up bored or unfulfilled in the role. I had to stop that unproductive cycle. I had to be clear about what I wanted and look at the bigger picture concerning my career. This time, I had to jump without a parachute and see where I would land.

How about you? Do you sometimes feel that you want to jump yourself? Are you a planner or go-with-the-flow type of person, or both? Maybe you might want to jump out of a job, but you are concerned that:

- You need to pay the bills, or
- You do not have enough money saved.
- You want to get necessary certification or training.

Who can blame you for thinking that way? I thought the same way too. As much as I wanted to jump, I had to take care of my family first. A person without a family has more flexibility to quit a job compared to someone who is responsible for a family. Before I made the jump, I made sure to have a discussion with my wife about the financial changes that were coming during my transition to a new

I came. I saw. I jumped!

career. I had to make sure that everyone was on board with the decision.

If you have a spouse or someone who could be directly affected by your job change decision, make sure to have a conversation with them beforehand. Look at your financial situation. How much available money in savings do you have? Can you manage with a smaller income for a short period? Do you have other income that you can use?

The good news is, you do not have to quit your job immediately to make a jump. You can do a mini-jump. By that, I mean you can consider your next career move while you are still working at your current job. You can try out a few activities you think you would love to do.

A mini-jump is like going to an ice cream store and sampling all the different flavors of ice-cream. Some ice cream will taste and look better than others. You will only commit to paying for those one or two flavors that taste the best. You can apply this same idea to approaching your career. Try different passions before fully committing to a particular one. When you jump, it doesn't have to be an "all or nothing" event. After all, you need to learn how to crawl before you can run. Here is a plan that can help you with your jumping strategy.

I came. I saw. I jumped!

ABC is as easy, as 1~2~3

Mountain climbers train before scaling a mountain. They work hard on conditioning themselves before a climb. Think of this ABC plan as your workout plan for your jump or mini-jump; think of it as an exit strategy for your career or job transition. I devised this plan from my observations of the career changes of other people as well as from my own experience. This ABC plan has three parts:

Analyze – your alternative self

Become – your new self

Create – your own job

Plan A: Analyze

The analyzing phase occurs as you plan your next job or career move while still working at your current job. You look at job opportunities or participate in job interviews for positions you are aiming for, and you network with people who are in these fields. This phase assumes that you already know your passion and life's purpose. The problem is that most people do not know their passion or purpose.

For this reason, you may not know how to begin your transition. You feel lost because you are stuck between a job you hate and an uncertain future. You are caught between a rock and a hard place. I was at that point for a long time, which is why I job hopped a lot. I was looking for that one job that would give me the fulfillment I craved, but to no avail. You see, this plan only works if you already know your passion and purpose.

"Vision without action is a daydream. Action without vision is a nightmare." - Japanese proverb

Plan B: Become

Plan B is the discovery stage. In this stage, you are looking to sample different passions or things you would love to do. It's like testing the water before diving in. There are two ways that you can go about doing this:

I. You could jump, and just quit your job, figuring things out along the way. This is what I did. It is risky, and you will need to analyze your financial situation and talk with your family who are dependent on you before using this approach. Do what feels right for you in your specific situation.

I came. I saw. I jumped!

II. The other option is for you to sample your different passions. Engage in activities where you get some exposure to different types of work that you think you might love to do while still working at your current job. This sampling could include freelancing, volunteering, an internship, taking courses, networking, etc. This experience allows you to get your feet wet, while at the same time maintaining that job security that pays your bills and accommodates your lifestyle.

As for my path, I started out with Plan A, which failed due to lack of clarity about my passion and purpose, so I then went for Plan B (I), and jumped. Sure, I could have carried on working at my old job before the jump and sampled a few activities to figure things out. That path would have been the smarter move. However, at that time, quitting felt right for me. At that time, I didn't know any other options, other than just burning all the boats. I either sink or swim.

Before you decide whether to jump or to go with your instincts, review your financial and family situation. Whatever you do, begin today to take some action towards work that you love.

Petros Eshetu

Abraham Lincoln once said, "I am a slow walker, but I never walk back."

The Founder and CEO of Amazon.com, Jeff Bezos, was one of many people who jumped from a good, well-paying job to start his business. Before starting Amazon.com, he had a lucrative position as a Senior Vice President for an investment firm on Wall Street. However, he had a passion for computers and he was looking to tap into the internet market in 1994 to start an online bookstore.

He was scared and worried about leaving his high-paying job to pursue his business idea. After talking with his wife, and getting her input and blessing to go forward, he started Amazon. Years later, after successfully selling books online, the company diversified its product lines. Now, Amazon is one of the largest companies in the world, and Jeff Bezos is now the fifth richest person on earth (Forbes Magazine). Just think, it all started because he decided to jump from a comfortable job to follow his dream. Consider:

- What would happen if you jumped?
- Could you be on the verge of creating something different that can help humanity move forward in a new way?

I came. I saw. I jumped!

Ways to test the waters

These are suggestions to help you take a mini-jump.

1. Finding Volunteering Opportunities

Try to take a couple of days or a week off, and volunteer in a field you might want to enter. Sample your passions. Volunteer at a library, a pet shelter, or any non-profit who's work interests you. You can find these opportunities online by searching the field of focus and search engines for volunteering, such as www. idealist.org.

You can also check to see if your current company has partnerships with non-profits in your area. I volunteered to help people with job coaching at a nonprofit education center through my corporate job. This experience was invaluable because it gave me insight into my future direction and a feeling of what it would be like to be in that role.

2. Networking

Ask family or friends if they know someone who's already in the field you're trying to enter. Join social media platforms like Facebook, LinkedIn or Google Plus to interact with people who have interests similar to your own. Get involved in the group discussion and connect with a few of them on a call or at a coffee shop near you.

When I began, I was nervous reaching out to new people for help or advice. I was not sure of what they might think of my request. The possibility that my request would be ignored made me nervous. Without regard for these emotions, I reached out, and I got responses. I ended up meeting people and coaches who gave me invaluable advice derived from their respective fields. I learned that people are more than willing to help if you just ask.

If you do end up connecting with some new people, here are some sample questions you may want to ask:

- How their day to day work feels?
- What made them choose their career path?
- What do they like or hate most about their job?

I came. I saw. I jumped!

- Are there any types of certification or specialized training needed to enter the field?

- Note: At the end of each meeting, you can even ask for a referral; someone they can introduce you to for more interviews.

Get as much information as you can during your meetings so that you can get a feel for the job and the career. The more details you get, the better your chance of envisioning yourself in that field and discovering whether you would like it or not. I recommend trying to talk to two or three people in your intended field to gather different perspectives.

When I considered career coaching, I talked to some career coaches in the non-profit sector, in a university setting and some who owned their coaching businesses. After every meeting, I sent a thank you email to each person I met for taking the time to talk to me, and I included one or two insights I gathered from the conversations.

3. Take a class/course

There are numerous online classes you can take in your chosen specialty. You can get a feel for your subject before pursuing it. The last thing you want to do is to invest in a certification or university degree only to realize halfway through that it is not what you want to do. I made that mistake when I invested in a two thousand dollar online course, and later realized it was not for me.

Part of my journey was starting an online blog and buying a webinar course to help me host webinars effectively. I bought into the message that webinars are key to getting maximum online traffic to my site, creating brand awareness, and making money. Even though this message is true, I didn't stop to think that I did not yet have a website, a product, or anything to sell. I had let my emotions get the best of me, and I was just so excited that I signed up without thinking it through.

By this time, the refund date had passed, so now I was stuck with this bill for a course that was of no value to me, at least not yet. The fact that I didn't have a job did not help.

This expense was unnecessary, and it hurt my pocket at the worst time. I learned a valuable lesson: Always have a vision and a plan in place before committing a huge investment into anything worthwhile. Locating a free or low-cost course, in the beginning, is best. Otherwise, use other strategies like networking or volunteering as low-cost alternatives.

Plan C - Create

I came. I saw. I jumped!

This section is where I answer the "starting all over again question." One day I had a call with my coach, Lindsey, on a week where I was struggling to make progress on my tasks. I was still writing my book while coaching on the side. I was trying to make money after leaving my job a few months earlier. The conversation:

Me: "I feel I must go back to the job market, the finance field, so I can start making money."

Lindsey: "Okay. You want to go back? How does that make you feel?"

Me: "I feel that if I go back to the finance sector, I will be a failure. I failed because I left that field so I can start a new life, but now I'm going back into it."

Me: "Coincidently, I'm writing a book about jumping to your dream career, but now I'm going back to what I was trying to avoid."

Lindsey: "Hmm, how does that make you feel? "

Me: "I feel like I'm an imposter. I don't have credibility by myself, or by helping other people leave for their dream jobs."

Lindsey: "Are you going back to the exact job, or same place?"

Me: "No, but it would be similar work to what I did previously."

Lindsey: "I see what you're saying. You just don't want to feel like a fraud? Like how do I keep my credibility if you go back to the same job at a different place?"

Me: "Exactly."

Lindsey: "What is it that you want to do? What is your passion? Talk to me more about that."

Me: "Well, I want to get into coaching. That's what I would prefer to do, but it's just hard to find a lot of jobs in this new field. Compared to finance jobs where you can find them everywhere. It seems like people who practice coaching start their own businesses".

Me: "I'm scared I won't find anything soon, so I feel like I need to fall back on something that I know well and is readily available."

Lindsey: "Is there any way you can be a financial coach?"

Me: (Pause) "I would love that!"

Lindsey: "Look at what you already know and your passion. How can you merge the two?"

Lindsey: "Is there a way to create your training ground. Is there a branch of finance that involves financial coaching? You have skills and abilities to do it. No need for you to reinvent the wheel."

I came. I saw. I jumped!

Me: "I guess I never saw like that."

Lindsey: "Yeah, start looking in your own field in a creative way. You already have a game plan. See this as a transitional period and training ground for the next step."

This conversation inspired me to create the Plan C in the ABC strategy. I had a belief that I was a failure because I went back to my previous field. That belief though was powerful enough to stop me in my tracks, and it prevented me from moving on to my goals.

Thankfully, I was only stuck for a day or two, and I had my coach for support. Some people are stuck in this mental space for weeks, months or even years. You might not even be aware of the self-sabotaging thoughts that stop you from acting on your dreams. Self-sabotage is the biggest reason most people do not quit a miserable job and die a life half-lived.

I learned a valuable lesson. There is no roadmap or script for a future career. Nothing is set in stone as to how things need to fall in place. My thinking had been narrow. I thought that finance was all I knew. I had to think big. I had to think outside the box.

Fear of failure stopped me in my tracks for a while. Then I had to stop and ask myself: "Am I truly a failure? What evidence is there to prove I'm a failure?" The truth is, I had discovered my gift and my purpose; I also had a game plan in motion. Do you need to start over again in your career? The short answer is no. Why would you? You have valuable skills that you have developed over the years both in your career and in your personal life. Although, I had to walk away from everything I was doing; there is nothing wrong with walking away and taking some of your previous experience with you as you leave.

Lindsey helped me think outside of the box about my career outlook. Why not create a new job for yourself using your unique talents and then add new skills to it? Have a "kill two birds with one stone" mentality:

- What base set of skills do you already have?
- What skills are you looking for in your next role?
- Is there a way for you to combine the two?

At some point, you might need to take a "two steps forward and one step back" approach in the event of a family emergency where you have to help pay bills. I would go back to my old job in a heartbeat and help if placed in that situation. I'm a responsible adult, and family always comes first. You also need to prioritize what's important. That does not mean that you must give up all of your dreams. You just need to delay them.

I came. I saw. I jumped!

Pay as you walk

I once read a story of an unemployed actor in Los Angeles who decided to get creative making money. He created a job where he got paid to walk with people in Los Angeles. Yes, that's right; he got paid to walk with people. I thought that story was insane too. This idea came to this actor while he was struggling to get roles. Like everyone else at first, he thought the idea sounded crazy. However, with time, he thought the idea made more sense. There are quite a few people that do not like to walk alone; they need a walking companion. Nowadays, with phones and computers, people are not connecting directly with others as much, or cannot coordinate schedules to meet.

When this actor first started getting paid to walk with strangers, he noticed that most people just needed someone to listen to their frustrations; the walk was therapeutic. Having their feelings acknowledged by another human being felt much better than just ranting on Facebook about a bad day. As a result, these people felt recognized and connected to others.

The last time I checked, this guy was charging seven dollars per mile for a walk, and he was working on creating an Ubertype app so that others could perform this service in other cities and countries. His mission is about motivating people to go outside and walk more. He is now called the "The People Walker." After hearing this inspiring story, I realized that I am in the wrong business.

Go big or go home

The best way for you to know if you're getting closer to your passion is by engaging in activities with people in your chosen field. Planning or thinking about your passion all day will not get you anywhere. You need to get a sense of the activity on the field to see if it aligns with your energy.

Maybe you want to work in an animal shelter, and then after enjoying your time spent playing with the animals, you find that you are not a fan of cleaning up the mess. When I started my self-discovery journey, my first thought was to be a career coach. I interviewed career coaches, and I also volunteered at nonprofits where I helped review resumes, cover letters, and helped with job interview preparation.

There were things that I liked and things I did not like about the career coach job. For instance, I realized that I could not stand

I came. I saw. I jumped!

looking at resumes all day. I'm good at fixing errors and making work history descriptions more appealing to employers, but for me, it is just not exciting after a while. I adjusted my path after this volunteer work, and I leaned more toward personal development coaching. My heartfelt mission was to help people gain clarity in their lives and to help them achieve their personal goals.

Changing identities

When you change your career, you are, to some extent, changing your identity. Let's say you have been known as Julie, the lawyer. You have spent ten years in the legal profession, and you're good at it. Then you decide not to practice law any longer. You quit your job, and now you are just Julie. Now, the question becomes, who is Julie?

Your personal identity is a very powerful determinate in defining who you are, and the actions you take. For example, if you identify as "I am fat" and "I have been fat and chubby all of my life" then you are not going to attempt to lose weight. Because by changing your weight you are essentially changing who you are. If you have been known as Bobby, the chubby bear guy your whole life, you will maintain that image until you decide to change how you identify yourself.

Now, if you change your identity to "I'm a body builder," and you truly believe it, then, you will raise your standards and actively learn how to be a bodybuilder. You'll learn how bodybuilders think, what they eat, and how they work out. You will read and study their habits and routines. You will take classes or learn from a bodybuilder fitness coach or a mentor. You do not need to change the physical world to see results; you just need to change your view of it.

In the past, I told myself I was an introvert. I am quiet, and I do not need a lot of friends; a few close friends would be enough for me. I remember when I was at work, I felt like I was invisible, and I never said more than I needed to. I was the type of person that just kept his head down and focused on his work. This behavior made building relationships within the company difficult and challenging. I was not adept at keeping up with all of the workplace politics.

Re-invent yourself.

I came. I saw. I jumped!

A career change is an identity change. You need to re-invent yourself and redefine your definition of success. Do you connect your self-worth with how much you make, or how much you help others? Selflessness can be more rewarding, I suggest you try to define success by how happy and fulfilled you are versus how much money you make. Strive for a mindset of not caring what others think. What's important is what you think of yourself.

When he changed careers, a good friend of mine, Eric said, "After nine years, I quit my job as an advisor because of the stress. I hated never seeing my family and working seventy-five hours a week, although I was making over six figures. I now teach business at a middle school level making thirty-five thousand, and I have never been happier."

Another friend, Tara, also left her comfortable corporate job to pursue her dream. She commented, "If I were ever to be happy I needed to take control of my circumstances. I could settle into a 'comfy' job that pays ok, or I could do something that I love. I chose happiness. I stepped out on faith, applied for a new job in a career that interests me and I got the job! I believe my happiness and peace of mind are invaluable. Never settle."

Petros Eshetu

These are examples of people that decided to go for what enriches their lives. They defined success in relation to their own values, and not on the values of others.

Public figures that have transitioned to different jobs in their long careers include:

- Martha Stewart – Sold investment securities on Wall Street before becoming a homemaking icon.

- Arnold Schwarzenegger – Was a bodybuilder before heading to Hollywood where he was one of the most famous actors before becoming California's Governor.

- Harrison Ford – Was a 15-year self-taught carpenter before becoming one of Hollywood's most famous actors.

- Al Franken – Was an established comedian, writer, and book author before running for public office to become a Minnesota Senator.

There is no roadmap for your future. Whatever direction you choose, make sure it's aligned with the authentic you. You might take Plan A, B or C. You might start out with one plan and then move to a different one. Maybe you jump, figure out your passion, and then end up returning to your old job to make some money so you can

I came. I saw. I jumped!

prepare for a second jump. Perhaps you need to take on odd jobs like delivering pizza, working in a grocery store or a restaurant to have an income during your career transition.

Understand that the work you do right now does not define or reflect where you will be in the future. Think outside the box and think big. Combine your existing talents and skills with your future aspirations.

It is important to have a vision. A vision will allow you to be creative in choosing how you can achieve your goals in ways that you otherwise would not have thought of. Knowing your destination allows you to create a new path. If you fail, keep trying again. Try a new method. Get over the fact that failure exists. I learned that nothing is set in stone about how I should move forward to reach my goals.

"The Dream is free, but the hustle is sold separately" - Unknown

Petros Eshetu

I came. I saw. I jumped!

Chapter 5

Do not let others keep you at the bottom of the mountain.

"Show me your friends and I'll show you your future" – *Christian Proverb*

If you can, try to befriend people who are at a point in their life that coincides with your goals. Learn their daily habits, and their talents will rub off on you. You will end up thinking like them and other successful people. You will think beyond your limited beliefs of what is possible. I heard a story from a motivational video about the power of the group:

It's like running a 100 Meter race. If you surround yourself with a group, where you are always winning (1st place), you won't put additional effort other than the bare minimum. However, if you run with a group where you always come last, you will put in extra effort to keep up and push beyond your comfort zone.

Will you feel bad, embarrassed or ashamed, like a failure? Probably! However, despite always coming in last in the group, your time in completing the race is much better than in a group where you always win. Measure performance by effort and not by the result. If you continuously work on improving yourself, your desired result will eventually materialize. You will hold the gold medal in your hand. You will write that book. You will start that new career.

Who you hang around with is a big factor in determining how successful you will be. The group will either push you forward beyond your limitations or keep you in your comfort zone. Do not connect your self-worth to an outcome, instead, associate it to the progress you are making. Make sure to always run your own race. After all, in life, you need to start from somewhere, right?

Your supporters

The people you hang around with will determine your success. Be careful not to surround yourself with negative people; "the life is too hard," or "I'm a victim of this world" complainers.

It's one thing to complain about the rain, snow or some bad weather. It is a whole other issue when you complain about

I came. I saw. I jumped!

everything under the sun. You know those people: People who are not grateful for what they currently have, and are always focused on what they do not have. I know them well because I used to be one.

I would hate my job and inevitably hate myself. This hate would obviously spill over to my relationships. I could see people receiving my negative vibe. People could sense it and would begin to distance themselves from me. I would meet a group of friends, and they could sense my negativity. They treated me differently because they could read my mind. I was emotionless with no smiles, only neutral facial expressions. My blank look was interpreted to be an indicator of a bad mood, but that was not always the case. The way I felt internally was reflected to the outside world. To solve this problem, I faked my smiles and laughter. It worked sometimes, but people could tell I was not always sincere. Later I learned that to change my outer experience I needed to change from within.

Slowly I changed and began recognizing gratitude every day in my life. I realized that life is too short not to enjoy it. Happiness is a choice. I began to attract people that I wanted in my life. Now I feel the negative vibes that others send. I now see my old self in them. When I see negativity in others, I am a bit more compassionate because I know how it feels.

Negativity feels like being in a pressure cooker. While the food inside is steaming and boiling on high heat, you dare not open the lid because you know that all of the food will explode into your face. You use a pressure regulator, a small nozzle located on top of the pot, to allow excess steam to escape. This pressure cooker example is similar to your life when you suppress all your pain, frustrations, and negative feelings and allow them to boil and cook inside. You just want to explode by lashing out at someone, but you know that won't turn out well. You need to use your escape nozzle to express your feelings calmly. Talk with a friend or a close confidant about any frustrations or negative emotions. This talk can be freeing and you will begin to attract the positive people in your life once again. It all starts with you.

Compadres

When you are taking this journey of self-discovery, you will need your compadres with you to push you to do better. You need to surround yourself with positive people that are ambitious and want to move forward.

I came. I saw. I jumped!

Joining groups will allow you to learn from each other and share ideas. Make sure to find groups that feel right to you. I once went to a networking group, and I will never forget what happened when I told them that I had quit my job to write my book and start a business. Their reaction was, 'isn't that's going to be hard" and "is that realistic?" Some just had that, "it will never happen" look on their faces.

I was surprised and taken aback. I mean, here I am joining a group, which I assumed was formed for mutual support, but all I heard was, "I can't do that." I felt lonely and isolated among the group after I opened up and shared my ambitions. I did not go back to that group.

Make sure you choose your community and groups wisely before committing. You want to join a group that has the same values, drive, and ambitions that you have. When the whole world is telling you not to do something, this is the group that will tell you to keep pressing forward.

Petros Eshetu

Birds of a feather, flock together

I paid my way to go to a group retreat in Provo, Utah. As a result, I got a chance to meet and associate with other like-minded people who also wanted to improve themselves and serve others more powerfully. This retreat consisted of people who were healers, coaches, book authors, entrepreneurs and others. Just speaking to them, experiencing their wisdom, and learning about their backgrounds was both infectious and mind-blowing. This retreat generated the positive energy that led me to write this book.

That experience changed my life's direction and allowed me to dream bigger than I ever would have imagined. I am now sitting in my room writing this book. Before that retreat, I never thought that writing a book would be possible for me. To quit my job and start a coaching practice was not in my immediate plan; it was a distant one. Surrounded by accomplished people and hearing their inspiring stories gave me the courage to know it is possible for me. After that weekend, I flew back to my home city Minneapolis with a new sense of energy and hope.

It is so important to go out and meet new people. Join different groups or create a support system to energize your move

I came. I saw. I jumped!

forward. Share stories and resources as you move in the same direction. You never know whom you might meet, or who may change your whole life path.

As the seasons change, so do your relationships

I expanded my social group beyond my normal circle of friends. I also abandoned the negative people in my life who were draining my energy. I had a friend who was always negative about everything. Instead of lifting you up, he would drag you down. If you were having a bad day, he always had the right words to make it even worse! He would always find a reason not to pursue his goals, and he would come up with reasons why I should not pursue my goals as well. The relationship became strained; every conversation drained my energy. I always felt like I was on trial to prove myself and justify my actions. It was though I was the victim and he was the judge with the wooden gavel. He just banged the table to silence me and give his final verdict: Guilty!

Don't get me wrong; I love him as a friend. He is a great guy when we are watching a football game together, but we are not on the same path. I have adopted this principle, "if you're not part of the solution, then you are part of the problem." We may have once traveled the same road, but now we are going in different directions.

I have learned that relationships with people change and mature over time. I have also learned that sometimes your friends become afraid of changes within the group dynamic. They see you pursuing your dreams, and they will take actions to prevent you from leaving the group or change the group's status quo.

If you put two live crabs in a bucket, both crabs will fight to climb out. As one crab starts climbing to make progress, the other crab rises to climb over it. Each crab pushes the other aside to reach the top. In the end, both crabs stay in the same bucket. It is the same with the negative people you hang around with. You try to leave the group, and they will find a reason to drag you back down. I would rather walk alone in the right direction than walk with others in the wrong one.

I came. I saw. I jumped!

Pain fuels your success

There are two motivators in life, pain, and pleasure. Of course, anybody would prefer to experience pleasure over pain to move forward. However, what I have learned from my experience is that pain is a much bigger motivator than pleasure. Pain tends to cut deep into your core. To experience pleasure, sometimes you first need to experience pain. After all, how can you appreciate one without experiencing the other?

If everyone were happy all the time, there would be little absolute change in our lives. The ups and downs of your life allow you to experience different emotional states. That is how you know you are living.

If you were just happy all the time, this would mean you do not require a conscious or unconscious effort to experience any different sensations. You would then have nothing to do and thus no need to think. In other words, not thinking would mean not existing. Here's an example.

Coming home from a failed first college semester in South Africa in 2004, I was at a low point in my life. The first time I was out of the house and living on my own was when I was in college. Away from home, I could do whatever I wanted without anyone looking over my shoulder. In the beginning, I found it difficult to meet new friends because I was a loner and an introvert.

Fear of rejection was running through my mind back then. I would routinely go to classes, then return to my room or go to the library to study for a couple of hours. On the next day, I would begin the cycle all over again.

To overcome these defects, I joined various activity groups on campus. Next thing you know, I'm going out to parties and bars. I went from having zero friends to having more friends than I could handle. I was not the talkative type, so I wasn't sure why they would even want to hang around with me. Later, I found out what they liked most about me was that I listened to them. They told me mostly about their girlfriend dramas or class stuff.

As the weeks went by with all the activities going around me, I began studying less and less. I began to lose the discipline to focus on my studies. I had lost my vision as to why I was even in college in the first place? I failed my final exams. During the semester break, I went back home to Harare, Zimbabwe. When I received my grades, I was terribly disappointed I had failed most of my classes or got an average grade at best.

I came. I saw. I jumped!

I thought, "I'm not good enough for school. I won't become anything substantial in my life. I had made my first trip out of the nest and fallen. As I sat in my room, depressed, lonely and feeling guilty for wasting the tuition money that my parents spent, I went deep within myself thinking: "Maybe I should not have gone to college. Maybe I should have just stayed at home and worked". These and other negative thoughts began running through my mind. I was spiraling out of control, and I did not want to leave my room for days. Then, out of nowhere, something beautiful happened.

I heard an inner voice say, "Get up and keep moving. Prove to everyone that it's your time now." It was the first time that I had heard my inner thoughts. I felt such clarity in my thinking. It was at that moment that I realized I would never want to go through that pain of failure or shame again even if that meant fighting my way back to become a better person.

I did not know it back then, but that decision and experience changed the whole course of my life. Those next few months, I worked my butt off to study as hard as I could, I studied fourteen hours each day to learn how to pass the SAT exam so that I could go to the United States and get a business degree.

Petros Eshetu

From the pain of failure, I learned the value of perseverance and making pain my friend. Pain gave me the jet fuel I needed to push myself to success regardless of any challenge in my way. I just bulldozed obstacles as if they were a joke. When I replaced my negative self-loathing thoughts with a positive motivational attitude, the wheels began turning in my favor. I reached my goal of coming to the United States, graduating, and then starting a life here.

You too can convert pain into achievement. Pain often results from failure.

- Failure not to be first place in the race.
- Failure not to climb that mountain.
- Failure not to start or succeed in that business.

In your life, if you can work through your pain by being patient and persistent, there is a lesson to be learned on the other side. The question is can you hold off long enough and not throw in the towel and just give up on your dreams? Can you be open enough to learn the lessons that are coming your way? Ask yourself these questions:

- Who are the people you spend time with?

I came. I saw. I jumped!

- Do they uplift you to move to a higher level, or do they drain your energy?

- Do they encourage you when you come to them with new ideas no matter what?

- Or do they tell you that what you have in mind won't work?

Do not be afraid to lose some friends or support from family on your way to surrounding yourself with the right people. You do not want to be the best person among an average group. You want to be an average person in the best group. The knowledge you gain from being surrounded by other people who have achieved the results that you seek will help you realize your own outcome. I would rather have two or three friends that support me than to have ten friends who do not contribute to my growth.

"The journey of a thousand miles begins with one step" - Lao Tzu

Petros Eshetu

I came. I saw. I jumped!

Chapter 6

If it didn't kill you, then it's time to live; creating goals and visions

You wouldn't believe what he said next. He said, "I'm running the race!"

This announcement was made by Cliff Young, a 61-year-old farmer in Australia after he decided to run in one of the toughest marathons in the world. The year was 1983.

Cliff was a simple guy, who wore overalls and work boots. He decided to compete in the toughest endurance marathon in Australia, spanning 543 miles and taking four to five days to complete.

The average competitors are 30 years younger than Cliff, and they are sponsored by large companies, like Nike, and they spend months training. Cliff had no prior marathon experience, and no athletic training regimen other than running around his farm and gathering sheep on foot because he could not afford horses or

Petros Eshetu

tractors. It usually took him two or three days to cover a two-thousand-acre plot rounding up two thousand sheep.

Before the race began, the other runners thought Cliff was a spectator, until he grabbed a number and lined up.

Everyone knew the race would take five days: everyone except Cliff. Historically athletes run eighteen hours, then sleep six hours and then return to running. Cliff was not aware of this established pattern. While all of the other athletes were sleeping, Cliff ran nonstop. Cliff did not run; he shuffled along.

In the morning of the second day of the race, all of the other runners were surprised to learn that Cliff had continued jogging all night. Cliff used this pattern throughout the course of the race, each night, Cliff got closer to leading the pack. On the final night of the race, Cliff surpassed all of the other athletes and won the race. Cliff also set a new course record for the Sydney to Melbourne marathon.

Today, Cliff's style of running is called the "Young-shuffle". Since 1983, at least three champions of the Sydney to Melbourne race have used the Young-shuffle to win the race. Cliff's victory produced another change: modern-day competitors do not sleep; winners must race all day and all night, just as Cliff Young did. When will you begin to run your race?

I came. I saw. I jumped!

Although preparation is usually important for racing, you do not have to prepare to pursue your dreams. You just need to start. Cliff, who had never run a race had nothing but belief in himself, and it worked. That's not to say that whatever you try will work out the first time, or go smoothly. The point is to get started.

"Now is not the right time," is an excuse. I have already addressed this notion at the beginning of this book. Believe me, now is the right time! There is no better time than the present. You may want to wait for the perfect time, but it will never come.

Richard Branson, the Founder of the Virgin Group, gives great advice to people who are holding back. He says, "If somebody offers you an amazing opportunity, but you are not sure you can do it, say yes – then learn how to do it later." I try to apply this "say yes" advice to my life every day.

A sparrow or an eagle

Whenever I think of a big vision or dream, and I have close friends who try to dampen my ambitions or tell me I cannot accomplish them, or that my dream is impossible, I think of two birds, the sparrow, and the eagle.

Petros Eshetu

Sparrows make a lot of noise all day, they fly low and only cover small distances. Eagles on the other hand, only make noise when it is necessary. Eagles fly at a higher level and travel longer distances than sparrows. These birds do not fly together. They never have and they never will. The people around you may not have a vision or goal to strive for. They are trying to enforce their beliefs on you.

- Are you the bird flying low or the one flying high?
- How is a sparrow going to tell an eagle how to spread its wings and fly?

That's why I choose to be an eagle and you can too.

An eagle is magnificent as a symbol of power and strength, the master of its destiny. That's why the eagle is the national symbol of the United States. Other nations also use the eagle as their symbol or coat of arms like Germany, Russia, Egypt, etc. The eagle has a majestic look and signifies long life and strength. These attributes are what you should strive for as you move toward your destination.

I learned about eagles when I went to an Eagle Center in Wabasha, Minnesota back in my college days. I learned how eagles have binocular vision and can see an object the size of a small rabbit

I came. I saw. I jumped!

from three miles away. Some of them, like the bald eagle, can fly as fast as one hundred miles per hour to catch prey. An eagle can catch and kill prey larger than itself. Now, I'm not saying for you to go out and kill all your enemies but rather to attack your big goals with force and determination. Have a crystal clear vision of what you want!

Your vision needs to be greater than your reality. Creating goals is easy but sticking to them is another story. There will be days when you want to quit or not act and do not feel like doing anything. That is when you need to have a compelling vision to pull you towards your goal. Have a strong reason why you want to achieve your goal. Make it the reason you wake up every morning.

I remember days when I did not feel like writing my book. I was exhausted, or I had writer's block. Focusing on my vision is what kept me going every time. I would visualize myself holding my book in my hand looking at the book cover, the title, the color, and flipping through the pages. I had to remind myself that I was writing this book to help and inspire others to chase their dreams. That is what consistently pushes me to keep moving forward. It is crucial to create goals and a vision for yourself.

Petros Eshetu

What is your fantasy resume? Visualize your life in 3-6 months. What does it look like? Feel it and write it here:

I came. I saw. I jumped!

Complete your vision

Step One

Write a one-page description of where you would like to be in your career and life in the next six months or year.

_____

_____

_____

_____

_____

_____

I came. I saw. I jumped!

Step Two

Look forward 3-5 years and have a vision of your ideal future.

Write a one-page description of where you would like to be in your career and life in the next 3-5 years.

_____

_____

_____

_____

_____

I came. I saw. I jumped!

Step Three

List the steps can you take immediately to begin turning your future vision into your current reality?

_____

_____

_____

_____

_____

_____

I came. I saw. I jumped!

Step Four

Prepare your 90-year-old birthday speech:

Write in the 3rd person, as if one of your friends is giving the speech. Allow yourself to see what you accomplished in your life and created on this earth:

_____

_____

_____

_____

_____

_____

I came. I saw. I jumped!

Petros Eshetu

Do not wait to be happy; choose to be happy now before you reach your goal or get that special job. Feel as if you have already attained your goal. Feel as if you have already reached the peak of the mountain. It is the journey up to the peak that is most satisfying, so enjoy the ascent.

It's not to say that the journey will be easy. There will be challenges. You will have setbacks. But once you reach the top, the view will be marvelous, and all of the pain and failure you went through along the way will have been well worth it.

Take your time creating goals and visions. For some of you, it may take a few hours, while for others, it could take days or weeks.

In the following chapters, I will cover some of the fears, challenges and mental blocks you may face on your climb to the top of the mountain.

I came. I saw. I jumped!

Petros Eshetu

I came. I saw. I jumped!

Chapter 7

Breaking loose, never looking back and embracing a mindset of freedom

"The hardest prison to escape is in your mind" –Unknown

Coach: "So what is the biggest goal you want to accomplish this year?"

Me: "I want to socialize more and network with people."

Coach: "Ok, what have you done so far?"

Me: "Um…. Nothing. I viewed a new social media website and came across a few groups I liked. I also found events I would like to attend, but I have not fully committed and joined a group yet."

Coach: "Okay, your homework is to attend one group event this week. We can touch base next week and talk about your experience."

One week passed

Coach: "So how did it go with the group event?"

Me: "I didn't go. I didn't have time to meet up with the group. It probably would have been boring anyway."

Coach: "Why would you say that? Isn't your primary goal to meet new people this year?"

Me: "Yes, I suppose."

Coach: "What stopped you then?"

Me: (short pause) "I wasn't sure they would like me?"

Coach: "Why wouldn't they like you?"

Me: "I don't know. I had a bad experience in the past, and I often feel uncomfortable in new social settings, especially in a group. Sometimes I think I am not very interesting to converse with. I fear they will see me as a fake and not want to talk to me."

Coach: "What is your biggest fear?"

I came. I saw. I jumped!

Me: "Rejection. I have been in group situations where I don't seem to fit in. At my old job, I was rarely invited to happy hour events, and I never knew why. Did I do or say something wrong? Some people treated me differently than others."

Coach: "Did you feel lonely or isolated from the group?"

Me: "Yes, I did. I am more comfortable being by myself, or with people I know well. I usually avoid making the extra effort to socialize with new people because I know I will feel awkward and the pain of rejection is hard to overcome."

The conversation I had with my coach was an awakening. I was surprised by the discovery that I feared meeting new people. The excuses I used only served to cover up a deeper problem, the paralyzing fear of rejection. I realized that the only way to begin to overcome this fear was by going to an event this week. No more excuses.

That same week I signed up for a Toastmasters group. On the day of the event, I almost talked myself out of going. "It's raining and cold outside, do I really want to go?", I asked myself. However, after some quick self-reflection, I grabbed my keys. As I bent down to put on my shoes, I felt the fear of the unknown rising inside me. My heart was racing.

I paused and took a deep breath. I grabbed my brown leather jacket, and I walked out the door. As I drove to the event, I repetitively told myself, "I can do it! I can do it!" I must have repeated that phrase at least 100 times before I arrived. As I pulled into the parking lot, I was very anxious, and my palms were sweaty.

Self-doubt began to creep in, and I thought, "I don't have to go with this. There is still time to turn back." This time I refused to turn back and I propelled myself out of the car and into the rain.

I entered the building and found my way to the conference room where six guests were already engaged in light conversation. As I found a seat, I could feel all eyes tracking me as I moved across the room. I wondered if they were happy to see me or if they thought: Who is this new kid on the block? I sat down and tried to be invisible.

The one-hour meeting passed quickly, and it was not so bad. I was introduced to everyone and even spoke in front of the group. That was a milestone for me. At the end of the meeting, I was so

I came. I saw. I jumped!

elated and proud of myself for venturing out of my comfort zone, that I decided to seek out additional networking groups.

What makes you sweat?

You may have self-sabotaging beliefs that prevent you from acting to get what you want. In this chapter, I will discuss "limiting beliefs" and how they affect us. I will use the terms limiting, negative or self-sabotaging beliefs interchangeably. Each term relates to negative thoughts that act as a roadblock to attaining goals. Only you can control your thoughts. Begin by focusing your mind on one item. The mind is a powerful player in changing your perspective on life.

The mind trap

This book is not a medical reference book, and I am not an expert in brain chemistry or Neurolinguistics Programming (NLP). However, I do have a basic understanding of how the mind is designed to help us succeed. Understanding the mind is important because how you view the world largely determines how you interpret events or experiences. Different emotions are evoked when you think about specific events. Emotions can help you act, or they can be a mental barrier to living a rich, and fulfilling life.

Understanding that your mind is designed to facilitate success will lead to results. Brian Tracy wrote an amazing article detailing the difference between the subconscious (or unconscious) and the conscious mind that I will introduce through this chapter. Brian Tracy is Chairman and CEO of Brian Tracy International, a company specializing in the training and development of individuals and organizations. His main goal is to help people achieve their personal and business goals faster and easier than they ever imagined possible. (www.BrianTracy.com)

The subconscious mind is similar to a memory bank. It has an unlimited capacity permanently to store everything that has ever happened to you. Its function is to store and retrieve data. It is designed to ensure that you do things the way you are programmed to do them, based on the beliefs and habits you have developed as your identity.

95% of your life is run by your subconscious mind.

I came. I saw. I jumped!

In the US News & World Report- Health and Medicine (2005), Marianne Szegedy-Masak wrote on the latest neuroscience research in regards to the power of the brain. She mentions in the report on how we are only conscious of 5% of our cognitive activity in our daily routine. In other words, 95% of most of our decisions, actions, emotions and behaviors are unconscious.

For example, walking is a habit. You learned how to walk at a young age through practice and repetition. If you had to relearn how to walk every day, your life would not be easy, and we would be in trouble as a species. You would never be able to go anywhere. Each day would be spent learning how to walk. Our subconscious allows us to internalize our habits, so we no longer must think about them as they become part of our daily routine.

Mental Programs we downloaded

As a child, you developed beliefs about the world around you. These beliefs can be negative or positive programs in your mind. You recorded everything your parents said and did. Think about when you were six years old, and your mother repeatedly said to you, "that's not good enough, you can do better." In your mind, you may have deciphered that interaction as negative and thought, "I'm not good enough" as a person rather than applying those feelings to that specific event or activity. Despite your mother's good intentions, your brain may process that advice as a fact in your memory regardless of whether it is true or not.

At such a young age, you are still building your memory bank of beliefs to set the foundation for your future identity. A shaky foundation can affect your future interpretation of the world around you. It may be 30 or 40 years later in your life, when you may realize that you are still running from that same old "I'm not good enough" mentality as you try to get ahead in life or pursue large goals.

For example, you may decide that you would like to start your own business, but then you think, "I will probably fail anyway, just as I have in the past." The negative belief program chimes in, telling you, "Of course you will fail, because you're not good enough."

Over the years, these negative programs in the mind become habits, and the mind applies them with very little thought. You then become an expert on not going for what you truly want in your life. You choose to play it safe. You may have had self-sabotaging thoughts for years without realizing them. Thus, it is not surprising

I came. I saw. I jumped!

that you do not want to quit that miserable job. Who can blame you, when you have these limiting beliefs tape recorder playing on 'repeat' in your head?

Thoughts are powerful. Even if the person who originally caused the formation of the limiting belief died many years ago, you will still play that tune in your head: The 'I'm not good enough' track. This negative thought can generate fear and doubt. Inevitably you stop trying to achieve your dreams.

If you can change your thoughts, you can change your reality. Imagine going for whatever you want. Imagine waking up every morning excited to see what the day brings. Imagine working hard for something that has meaning to you. This reality is possible for anyone.

Find the weeds in the mind

"When you change the way you look at things, the things you look at change" -Wayne Dyer

Another way to think of the subconscious mind is to see it as a garden with rich fertile soil. The conscious mind is the gardener who plants seeds to cultivate and grow. Each plant in the garden represents a belief program that was planted a long time ago. The plants can be flowers or weeds. Some have deeper roots than others. Flowers represent good beliefs (like treating everyone with respect). Weeds are the negative beliefs ('I cannot do it'). To have a beautiful, healthy garden, you need to have more flowers and fewer weeds. Plants bloom better when there are fewer weeds.

In school, I took an agriculture class, and I learned about plants and farming. My semester project was to grow green beans in the school garden. I learned about plants and how weeds can steal the water and important nutrients away from the desirable plants. If you do not remove weeds regularly, your plant will die in the garden. The same can be said about beliefs. If you do not remove those limiting beliefs, you will stop moving forward and will not reach your full potential in life.

What tune is running your show?

So how do you know if you have limiting beliefs playing in your mind? The answer is simple. The activities you like will come easily to you because you have mental programs that support and welcome them.

I came. I saw. I jumped!

The opposite is also true. If you find difficulty with the activity that you require to achieve, you have mental programs that do not support that goal or the activity required to achieve it.

So how do you remove a negative belief? The first step is to be aware that it exists. You have already won half the battle by simply acknowledging the limiting thought. After all, you cannot fight an enemy that you cannot see.

You can replace your self-sabotaging beliefs with new beliefs that are more positive; beliefs that encourage you to keep striving forward. Remove the weeds in your mind garden and a positive seed will grow in its place. However, before you can remove the weeds, you must find them.

Journaling is a fantastic way to organize your thoughts and differentiate between the flowers and the weeds. If you have never written your thoughts in a journal, now is a great time to begin. I have journaled regularly for a couple of years now, and it has been beneficial in helping me clarify my thoughts and feelings. Placing my thoughts on paper (or computer) allows me to see my problem areas better, and to come up with a plan to solve these problems. It can be a stress reliever, especially if you cannot speak to someone about your challenges.

Questions for reflection include:

- How was I feeling when I had the thought of doing a specific task/goal?

- What fears or beliefs might be stopping me?

- What is the worst thing that could happen if those fears come true?

Probe; ask yourself these questions. Think critically. Speak with a trusted friend or coach. They may be able to help you identify what's going on, and give you the perspective that you need.

Once that you are aware of the negative programs, you can then begin the removal process. In other words, once you see the weed, you can remove it, and replace it with a new seed.

For the new seed to grow, you may need to get your hands dirty. You need to put forth the effort to reap the reward. You must dig into the soil, add the seed, place the soil on top and water the seedling daily for it to become a plant and grow. You need to act to breakthrough into the subconscious mind and make a lasting change.

I came. I saw. I jumped!

This action is done through habit and repetition. The subconscious is a habit mind; that is how it learns. There is no way around it.

Actively pursue your goals, whether that means doing research on your possible activities or taking a course on a topic you might be interested in pursuing. Additionally, you need to repeat positive self-talk to yourself every day, so the seed (positive program) is planted in your mind. When you repeat a phrase out loud to yourself multiple times, you find yourself beginning to believe it. If you begin each day by saying, "I am enough, and I love my imperfect self," you will begin to slowly replace the "I'm not good enough" limiting thought.

Get comfortable being uncomfortable

The subconscious mind wants you to keep thinking and acting in a manner consistent with what you have done and said in the past. Your habits of thinking and acting are stored in your subconscious mind (garden). It has memorized your comfort zones, and it works to keep you in them.

That is why sometime you maybe emotionally and physically uncomfortable whenever you attempt to do anything new or different, or when you begin to change an established pattern of behavior. You can feel your subconscious pulling you back toward your comfort zone each time you try something new. Even thinking about doing something different from what you are accustomed to will make you feel tense and uneasy.

This concept is important because when you decide to jump, your subconscious will attempt to dissuade you. It will be rough in the beginning, as you push yourself past your comfort zone. You must be willing to give in to the feelings of awkwardness and discomfort when doing new things. With anything new in life, it is often difficult to begin.

"He who says he can and he who says he cannot are both usually right" - Confucius

It only takes about ten minutes to create a new belief. You need to back it up with actions and habits to sustain lasting change. The more you practice, the better you become, and the faster the new belief becomes a habit.

I came. I saw. I jumped!

In the next chapter, I will share some clearing techniques that I have found useful to help remove my mental blocks (or weeds).

- What fears or limiting beliefs are holding you back from your dreams?
- What situation or interaction caused the belief?
- What would you rather believe?
- Who would you be without that belief? How would you feel?

Petros Eshetu

I came. I saw. I jumped!

Chapter 8

Landing on your feet and how to stay there; clearing techniques

For the longest time, I suppressed my negative feelings. A lot of my suppression had to do with feelings of shame. The shame of being my real self rather than a perfect me (a people pleaser). This started from childhood because I was an overweight kid. Other kids bullied me much of time. My playmates would make a lot of fat jokes about me.

I remember kids calling me 'Yokozuna' who was a popular fat sumo wrestler on television back then. Being called names like that was hurtful and very painful at that time. I never felt so ashamed of being me. It was as if the fear of living in my own skin produced a choke hold on my neck; I struggled for every breath; my face turned red as my veins popped out.

I came. I saw. I jumped!

I began to experience life-numbing pain and the feelings of shame. I did not know it at the time, but when I numbed my negative feelings, I also numbed my positive feelings, because I was cutting out their source which was my soul. I never allowed myself to be vulnerable in front of others unless they were a part of my family or close friends. So, I found it difficult to connect with other people. More importantly, I found it difficult to connect to my authentic self.

Maintaining this fake persona, the "Mr. Perfect image," was energy draining and stressful. However, once I let go of the shame by exposing it, the pressure of trying to be perfect miraculously disappeared. My fear of being judged or making mistakes reduced significantly. Eventually, I stopped dwelling on what others thought about me and began to care what I thought of myself. What others thought of me became irrelevant. I decided to be grateful for who I was. I felt like I lost a huge weight from my shoulders. No longer did I need to wear a mask to hide who I was.

Clearing

Clearing is removing limiting beliefs from your mind; removing weeds and planting new seeds in their place. I will introduce different clearing methods that you can apply immediately. Think of these clearing methods as alternative ways to water the garden so that new plants can begin to grow. Just like you can water the garden using sprinklers, a bucket, hoses, and so on.

If you're fearful or unhappy about something in your life, you need to dig deeper into the roots and figure out why you feel that way. Why do you have such a reaction? Not everyone will react the same way you do. You might be in a room with four people, and one person might say something that makes your blood boil. You blame the person who said it, for making you angry. But if the other people in the room did not react as you did, then how could he or she have made you angry? Why doesn't everyone feel the same way? What belief is playing in your head? What negative thoughts do you tell yourself? It is those thoughts that generate your negative emotions.

I came. I saw. I jumped!

Check yourself on how you are feeling throughout the day. Are you happy, sad, angry, nervous, mad, disappointed or even ashamed? Write down how you feel whenever you feel some negativity. Once you expose a feeling, you will become more aware of it. Once you are aware of it, you can then begin to resolve it. Attacking an enemy in light is much better than attacking in darkness.

Why is this important? If you do not deal with an underlying negative issue head on, it will continue to be a problem, and it will keep blocking you from acting toward your goals. Those negative thoughts have negative emotions attached to them. They may return in an hour or a few hours, or weeks, or months, or years later. You can try to brush them aside or try to forget about them. But those measures will only provide a temporary solution. The best way to solve this problem is to tackle it head on. Get your hands dirty in the garden, find those weeds and pull them from their roots.

Here are some examples of clearing methods:

1. Awareness

2. Mantra

3. Time Management

4. Gratitude

5. Visualization

6. Drawing

7. Motivational Posters

1. Awareness- being aware of the mind trap, a slave at heart

Being aware of the negative programs is half the battle. When you have a set goal for a period of time, but nothing ever gets done. Make sure you journal this situation somewhere.

- Ask yourself why you have not acted; what is stopping you from acting?

I came. I saw. I jumped!

- Are you struggling to manage or prioritize your tasks efficiently? Do you need to reduce your workload to smaller manageable chunks?

- Is there a belief that is stopping you from moving forward?

Remember, you want to expose what it is that is stopping you from acting. As I mentioned in previous chapters, talk to a trusted colleague or friend who can give you invaluable insight into your issue.

I believe there are two sides to jumping in the thought process. There is a bright side and a dark side of jumping as seen below.

Jump Scale

Bright side	Dark side
Just	Junk
Understand	Underneath
My	Misery
Passion	Poison

Throughout the day you will have many random thoughts. Sometimes you lean toward the brighter side, and others times you favor the dark side. How do you know which end of the scale you're on? It will depend on which side you focus your thoughts on at that moment. If you focus on negativity, then you're on the dark side. If you focus on positive thoughts, then you're on the bright side. You may think you do not have control over your thoughts, but you do.

For example, let's say you're on a diet and you keep telling yourself,

"I hate eating these carrots."

"I'm starving myself. "

"This is a waste of time."

"I'm always hungry. I will never lose weight. Why should I suffer?"

More than likely you're on the dark side, and most likely you will end up going for the donut, or whatever sweet junk food is around. You feel hopeless to have that body you want. You feel pain and want some pleasure (comfort) foods. Pain is a sign that

I came. I saw. I jumped!

you're growing and getting out of your comfort zone. You are learning something new. It's a sign of progress and not a failure.

Another way you could tell yourself in a similar scenario is:

"*Wow, I'm so proud of myself.*"

"*I feel stronger. I feel healthier.*"

"*I'm learning to control my appetite and hunger.*"

"*Every day I'm getting closer to my ideal weight.*"

"*I am going to eat an apple or drink some water instead.*"

Do you notice the difference between the two responses in the diet scenario? Both sets of statements are equally powerful, but they work in opposite directions. By that I mean the first sets of statement generates negative emotions (anger, frustration, self-pity, hopelessness, etc.). The second set of statements generates positive feelings (happy, excitement, hopefulness, etc.). You maybe believe that all of the thoughts in your mind are true, but they are only true if you make them so. However, you can control your thoughts, and it starts with the direction of your focus.

2. Mantra-repeat it till you believe it

Once you expose the negative mind script, you want to replace that limiting belief with a positive one. The way to move from the dark side to the bright side of the jump scale is to overwhelm your mind with positive phrases to combat the negative.

Remember the only way to make an impression on the subconscious is through habit. Practice repeating positive phrases daily, so it makes a print and adds new beliefs in your mind. Water the seed so it grows. When the "I'm not good enough" song starts playing in your head, respond with:

"You know what, I am good enough. I am love. I am deserving. I am worthy. Yes, I can do it."

Self-affirmation statements can be as short, or as long you want them to be. An example of a longer version option could be:

"You know what, I am good enough. I am love. I am deserving. I am worthy. I am the captain of my ship. Every day I am getting closer to my goals. I am getting closer to my dreams. I

I came. I saw. I jumped!

am learning something new, and I am challenging myself whenever I can."

Create your own personal mantra that you can use throughout your day. Mantras help you get centered, but they are not a means to avoid negative feelings. In fact, it is the opposite. You want to first bring to the surface whatever feelings you are experiencing and acknowledge them. Do not hide them. It is okay to sit with them for a while, but do not get stuck there too long! Once you acknowledged your feeling, begin to use the mantras to help move you forward in the right direction. Try to find your balance.

Below is a helpful guide to show you how to create a mantra.

Step 1

What do you want? This question tends to stump people because they do not know what they want, but they always know what they do not want. So, it might be counter-intuitive, but the best way to answer, "What do I want?" is to answer an alternative "what is it that I do not want" in my life?

List 5-10 things you do not want in your life. For example,

- I do not want a miserable job.
- I do not want a bad relationship.
- I do not want to be a failure.
- I do not want to be broke.
- I do not want to hate in my life.

Step 2

Once you have completed the list in step 1, reverse all your statements, so that each one becomes the opposite statement. For example,

- I want a great job.
- I want a wonderful and loving relationship.
- I want to be a winner.
- I want to be wealthy.
- I want love in my life.

I came. I saw. I jumped!

Step 3

Change what you do want, in otherwords replace the 'I want' with 'I am' at the beginning and change the sentence structure when necessary.

- I am loving my job.
- I am in a loving relationship.
- I am a winner.
- I am wealthy.
- I am love.

"I am" is one of the most powerful statements you can make. It's a message that gets sent directly to your subconscious mind, where it records whatever you say as a fact. Whatever follows the 'I am' statement, will begin the creation of whatever it is you want to appear in your life.

Anything you focus your attention on grows. You can write your mantras on a post-it note, or record them on your phone so you can hear them anytime.

Another trick I've used is to create a playlist of motivational songs and or speeches that I save on my I-phone so I can to listen to them later. Whenever I feel low or unmotivated, I would begin to listen to these inspirational messages and soon I would be motivated to act. For example, I am a big fan of Les Brown, who is a successful entrepreneur and motivational speaker; I always listen to his speeches to lift me up. I listen to Les while I am running, working out, cooking or driving.

Keynote:

Positive thoughts lead to positive feelings, which in turn lead to positive emotions such as hope, joy, gratitude, excitement, and inspiration. Positive thoughts are motivation for action.

Negative thoughts lead to negative feelings, which in turn lead to negative emotions such as shame, fear, doubt, anger, frustration, and inaction.

I came. I saw. I jumped!

3. Time management

One of the biggest challenges for people, either before or after the jump, is time management. It was a huge challenge for me. My never-ending to-do lists caused a great deal of my stress. I had difficulty setting boundaries for myself, so my to-do lists kept getting longer; they never ended. Once I made the jump, I thought I would have more time to get things done. I did acquire a bit more time, but I also realized that I needed to be more efficient with my time management. What you do with your time is important.

I began to write my goals and describe my vision for my life again. Then, whenever I created my to-do list, I would look to see if these tasks brought me closer or further away from my goals. These judgments helped prioritize my tasks for the day. You need to block time throughout the day for fun, for business, for working, for studying and learning, for friends, for exercise and so on.

When I first quit my job to examine what I really wanted to do, I only focused on my book and my blog all day while neglecting other areas like health and relationships. It is easy to become a workaholic again. As a result, my stress returned. There is a consequence to being burnt out and not having the proper time to rejuvenate and refresh your body and mind. The best way to avoid burnout is to plan your day in advance or the night before.

Remember, what good are successes if your health is deteriorating? What good are successes if you do not have family and friends to share in your achievements?

To maintain my balance, I apply 3-4 actions below in my daily routine:

- I exercise three or four times each week for 30 minutes.

- I eat meals at home with sufficient quantities of fruits and vegetables.

- I drink at least five or six glasses of water each day.

- I get seven or eight hours of sleep each night.

- I meet with one or two friends each week or make new friends by networking.

I came. I saw. I jumped!

- I plan my day in advance.

- I meditate each day.

- I make a list of five things for which I am grateful for.

- I read a book.

- I research a new field online or in a book.

- I have fun and relax.

Try to set aside time for your activities every week; It is all about developing good habits. For example, at 7:00 am you might exercise on Monday, Wednesday, and Friday for at least thirty minutes. Keep at it. Have your gym or workout clothes already laid out, so you do not have to decide what to wear on the next day.

Take it a step further, plan the exercise routine and your meal on the day before they are scheduled. It will be difficult at the beginning but try to set up a routine. Eventually, with repetition, your routine will become a habit.

4. Gratitude is an attitude

Petros Eshetu

Simple gratitude can lead to happiness. Be grateful for what you already have in this moment of your life. Focus on the abundance of life, not the scarcity. I keep a gratitude journal. I wake up every morning, and I write down three to five things for which I am grateful.

Each one can be as simple as:

- "I am grateful for the warm cup of coffee."

- "I'm grateful for my friend Bob returning my phone call."

- "I'm grateful for finishing my writing work yesterday."

Gratitude is a ray of energy to give a powerful start to your day. In the beginning, I found it difficult to write down my gratitude list. Some days I would write, while on other days I would be too lazy, tired or just not feel up to it.

Soon, I began to notice a difference on the days when I wrote my gratitude list in contrast to the days I did not. On days when I wrote my gratitude list, I tended to feel good throughout the day and not so stressed. However, on those days when I did

I came. I saw. I jumped!

not write my gratitude list, I would be unbalanced and anxious. Slowly I began to write my list three times a week. Then in a few weeks, I added a day or two, and then I made a daily gratitude list four or five times each week. Now I do it every day.

Not only has a gratitude journal kept me grounded and content with my life, but my list has also allowed me to appreciate the smallest things, and to enjoy the present moment. My stress and discontent have gone down significantly. Try if for yourself. See what happens, and remember: The biggest key to happiness is not money, but gratitude.

5. Visualization

Visualization is so important because you need to see your future in your mind to believe you can attain it. Once you have this belief, a picture will be created in your mind. An important step that alot people miss when they visualize is the feeling that they have already attained their goal.

Some people make a big mistake by waiting to accomplish a goal before they start to feel good. I made this same error for many years. I learned that I need to be happy now. You want and need to feel good during the time you are seeking your goals. Once you achieve the goal, you will feel a brief sense of accomplishment and amazement. Eventually, you will move on to the next goal.

Many athletes and successful people practice visualization before a game or an event. Think of successful people like Michael Jordan, Tiger Woods, Oprah Winfrey, Jim Carrey and others. Not only can visualization help you improve your performance through the power of focus, accuracy, and motivation, but visualization also can help reduce fear and anxiety, by envisioing the future event.

Create a mental picture by adding as many details as you can about an occasion when you realize that you have achieved a goal. What are you wearing? Who is around? How do you feel?

A vision board will help with your visualization.

I came. I saw. I jumped!

How to create a vision board

- Write the goals you want to achieve over the next year or two.

- Go to a magazine or online and find a few inspiring pictures that you believe should be in your imagination of the occasions that portrays each of your goals.

- Get some cardboard or poster board that is large enough to accommodate all of your pictures.

- Get any other supplies you need like scissors and glue

Begin to make a masterpiece of your dream life. Add pictures and small descriptive phrases underneath each goal. After you finish, begin to review your vision board regularly. I look at my vision board every morning before I begin my day, so I have my goals alive in my mind throughout the day and I do not lose my focus on priorties.

6. Drawing

Along with the vision board, you could draw a picture of your future life. There is an inner child in all of us to help us draw. Draw your current and your future life on the next page. For example, if you want a specific body shape, draw where you are now and then draw your dream body. Have fun!

For example*:* Dream 1- I want to be slimmer, and to have a six-pack by December 2017.

I came. I saw. I jumped!

Current life   Future Life

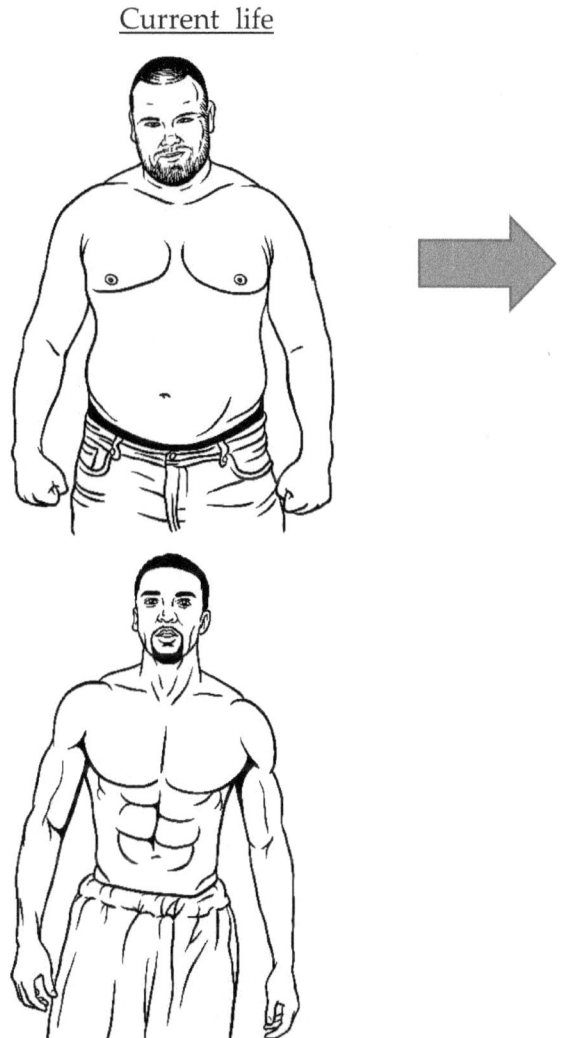

Petros Eshetu

Dream 1-_____

Current life   Future Life

I came. I saw. I jumped!

Dream 2-_____

Current life   Future Life

Petros Eshetu

Dream 3-_____

Current life  Future Life

I came. I saw. I jumped!

7. Motivational Poster

You can also create a poster that motivates you. You can have posters with inspiring words or phrases that you can place around the house or office. If you ever you need an inspirational message, I recommend getting the Holstee Manifesto poster (as seen on the next page). You can also find it at www.holstee.com. This poster has inspired thousands and even millions of people to take inspired action towards their dreams, including me.

Petros Eshetu

THIS IS YOUR LIFE.
DO WHAT YOU LOVE, AND DO IT OFTEN.
IF YOU DON'T LIKE SOMETHING, CHANGE IT.
IF YOU DON'T LIKE YOUR JOB, QUIT.
IF YOU DON'T HAVE ENOUGH TIME, STOP WATCHING TV.
IF YOU ARE LOOKING FOR THE LOVE OF YOUR LIFE, STOP;
THEY WILL BE WAITING FOR YOU WHEN YOU
START DOING THINGS YOU LOVE.
STOP OVER ANALYZING, **LIFE IS SIMPLE.** ALL EMOTIONS ARE BEAUTIFUL. WHEN YOU EAT, APPRECIATE EVERY LAST BITE.
OPEN YOUR MIND, ARMS, AND HEART TO NEW THINGS AND PEOPLE, WE ARE UNITED IN OUR DIFFERENCES.
ASK THE NEXT PERSON YOU SEE WHAT THEIR PASSION IS, AND SHARE YOUR INSPIRING DREAM WITH THEM.
TRAVEL OFTEN; GETTING LOST WILL HELP YOU FIND YOURSELF.
SOME OPPORTUNITIES ONLY COME ONCE, SEIZE THEM.
LIFE IS ABOUT THE PEOPLE YOU MEET, AND THE THINGS YOU CREATE WITH THEM SO GO OUT AND START CREATING.
LIFE IS SHORT. LIVE YOUR DREAM AND SHARE YOUR PASSION.

"THE HOLSTEE MANIFESTO" ©2009   WRITTEN BY DAVE, MIKE & FABIAN   DESIGN BY RACHAEL   WWW.HOLSTEE.COM/MANIFESTO

I came. I saw. I jumped!

There are so many other clearing techniques that you can use to help remove your limiting beliefs. I highly recommend the Ho'oponopono practice which is an ancient Hawaiian clearing technique that I use where I practice forgiveness as part of my healing to my old wounds. You can also try the Tapping method, Meditation, Yoga, the Passion Test (by Janet and Chris Attwood), Self-compassion and so much more. Try different techniques and see which ones works best for you.

Petros Eshetu

I came. I saw. I jumped!

Conclusion

The scorching rays of the sun came down upon me as I prepared to jump to that next boulder. I could feel myself getting a dark tan; my mouth was dry, and I was thirsty. My skin was now burning. I felt as though I was being prepared as the next meal for the hungry boulder. Without realizing that I was placing one foot after the other, I began to move forward.

My walk turned into a run. Before I knew it, the ground under my feet disappeared, and I was airborne for a second or two. Suddenly, I had solid ground beneath my feet. I had made it to the other side. With a smile on my face, I breathed a big sigh of relief, and I tried to catch my breath. I got a few bruises on my knees, but I did win the final mental battle.

As I stood and looked up, I could see the contrast between where I was now and where I had been. The boulder I had jumped was bare. The one that I landed on had flowers scattered with green, red, yellow and brown colors. The air was refreshing with various perfumed scents; I filled my lungs with the different fragrances. I stood still; I took in the view and remained present in the moment. There was an aliveness in the air. In the distance, I could see stairs leading down to the lower level of the boulder.

We will all need to jump out of a bad situation and into a new one. This situation could involve a relationship, business, job, project, etc. I leanred that making a jump is more of a mental challenge rather than a physical one. It is a mind game that you fight against your own inner critique. Negative self-talk breeds the fear and the doubt.

"When life throws you lemons, make lemonade."

You may be stressed, bored, or burnt out. This condition may be the result of work that you do not want because you're not passionate about the job, or because you do not use your natural gift to perform the job. Your anxiety could also result from using your gift, but applying it in the wrong vehicle. You want to change your career, but you do not know where to begin. I know the feeling because I was there for a few years. I was stuck in a rut for the longest time until I reached a crossroad. I reached a point where I could not take it anymore, and I needed to make a change. What was once a should-do list is now a must-do list.

I came. I saw. I jumped!

We are conditioned to have a plan in life before making any drastic changes, especially when it comes to jobs, where that drastic change impacts your livelihood. The sensible option is to have a backup plan, but conditions will not always permit that luxury. At times, you're going to have just to jump, which is what I did. I have had no regrets, and I have found my true calling. This experience is part of what inspired me to write, *I Came. I Saw. I Jumped!*

Of course, not everyone can make a jump immediately. Each of us has our responsibilities to other people. We need to help take care of the bills and spend time with loved ones. However, you can still take small steps forward. Figuring out your gift and working on it can give you a sense of satisfaction that enables you to know which activities give you energy and make you feel alive.

In my opinion, you will never have a fulfilling life if you do not use your natural born gift every day to help others. It is also worth repeating that passion is a journey and not a destination. It is important to enjoy the ride!

Now, can you be successful without being passionate about what you do? Sure, this happens all the time, but I believe you will never reach your full potential if you do not do what you love. On the other hand, there may be people who are living their passion and doing what they love but are not regarded as successful according to some peoples definition because they are either not wealthy or they do not have trophies or awards. In the end, however, only you can determine what success means. The outcome is not as important as the progress you make and the growth you experience towards your fulfilled self.

Family

Many of your beliefs about your career come from your family, your culture or a trusted advisor or teacher. Many chronological goals (going to school, getting a degree, getting that respectable stable job, getting married, buying a house, having kids, retiring from a high paying job) were planted by well-meaning adults long before you were making your own decisions. The good news is that it does not have to be that way now. You can take ownership of your own destiny.

This book is about taking responsibility for your life. If you do not like something, you have the obligation and responsibility to figure it out and take action to correct it. Be your own inspiration.

I came. I saw. I jumped!

No pain, no gain

Part of the formula for your success includes pain and failure. I know, because I went through it. There is no escaping it. Many times, I was disappointed or wasted time and money in going down a wrong path. I learned many hidden lessons as I gained clarity about my purpose. I used that pain as the fuel for my driver to keep me going forward. Some people might not grasp what you're doing. Your actions will not make sense to them, and that's okay. Only your understanding, not theirs is important. If you know what you're doing and why you're doing it, you will not allow the opinions of other people to sweep you off your path. Never forget to spread your wings and fly like an eagle. Let the sparrows find their own way back home.

Career identity change

It's challenging to change a career because it involves changing your identity. This change is not an easy or straightforward process, but rather a steady, gradual conscious change. You slowly give up the old image that you spent years building, and a new you emerges.

There will be doubts, uncertainty, and questions along the way to your identity change. When you make a jump, you may feel like you have lost your footing. There will be uncertain times when you fear the unknown. If you hold on, you will eventually find firm footing. Once you know your gift, and once you find the right vehicle to transport it, you will be on your way to serving others in a deep and impactful way.

When is the best time to jump? The best time is now. It can be one large jump or a series of small mini-jumps. Apply the ABC exit strategy to help you transition in your jump. Begin by testing the waters before making a one hundred percent commitment to your next career direction.

Apply what feels right. Perhaps you will discover something totally different than you anticipate. Make sure your activities push you forward toward meaningful work that makes a difference in your life. This activity will give you fulfillment not the money, houses or cars.

Finding your passion is finding your journey. Try different activities or jobs that you think you might love to do. This journey will take you out of your comfort zone, and you will meet new people along the way.

I came. I saw. I jumped!

This period of self-discovery and experimentation can be as long or as short as it needs to be for you. Everyone's path will be different. Starting is what's important. Determine which activities create energy within you, and which ones drain your energy. Keep a record of these activities.

Do more of the activities that light you up, and adjust your path as needed. Remember, nothing is a failure; it is only feedback to teach you which paths to take and which ones to avoid.

To be successful and to stand out, you need to love what you're doing. The best way to stay true to yourself is to embrace your unique qualities and strengths that allow you to hone your craft and become an expert at what you do. Your competitive advantage will come forward.

No script to your life

There is no script for life as you move forward. You are creating the moment as you move along your journey's path. Again, there is nothing set in stone about the path you need to take.

In Hollywood, scripts are written after journeys are completed. Take the jump and begin to write your own Hollywood story; a blockbuster script of your life!

Gather your compadres

Surround yourself with a supportive group that can take you beyond your own limits. Learn their habits. To be the best, you're going to have to copy the best. I found my comrades: writers, entrepreneurs, and authors at a single retreat.

These compadres so inspired me that I gathered the courage to write this book. In conversations with them, I learned the habits and strategies of the most effective ways to write. I learned from their mistakes and lessons. I used their roadmap and along with a coach, I wrote a book in three months, not three years as I originally thought.

Maybe fear or limiting beliefs are blocking you. The belief that you are not good enough or that you are not special or that you are too old. Maybe you want to quit your job but later talk yourself out of quitting. You start telling yourself that this job is not that bad after all, even though deep down, you know that the job has no meaning for you. You feel miserable. You may start

I came. I saw. I jumped!

making excuses: "I'm broke, or how will I pay my bills?" To avoid minor steps forward to find work that you would love. It's up to you to control what thoughts you let influence you.

Apply the clearing techniques and other strategies that are suggested in this book to remove your self-sabotaging beliefs. Replace your old, negative beliefs with new ones. Take small actions every day towards your goals. Make it a habit to reinforce your mind to focus on things that matter most. Be grateful for what you have. Live a life of abundance, not scarcity.

When you write down what you want in your life, you are sending an intention into the universe. Nothing in life ever began without intention. Therefore, creating clear goals and a vision is important. This creation gives you a target. Take the inspired action whenever you receive a great idea. You may be inspired to visit a specific website, or read a certain book, or join a class or a program or create a business idea.

When you get that inspiration, do not brush it aside, act on it. Do not let it pass you by; you might not get it again. And remember, there is no right or wrong approach. There is only your own, unique approach. You need goals and vision to pull you towards your dreams. The "what" and the "why" are more important than the "how."

Final note

Jumping isn't easy. If it were easy, then everyone would do it. It will probably be one the most difficult things you will do in your life. Will you get hurt or experience pain? Yes. Will you fail? Maybe. Will you have a pretty landing? Not always. But you will never know unless you jump. I went through a long period of self-doubt and uncertainty before finally finding my passion and purpose. It is all part of the discovery process, and I can tell you, it is well worth it in the end.

There were days, as I wrote my book, where I questioned myself. "Am I good enough to write this book? I am not special. There are already lots of books with similar topics from well-known authors. Why would anyone want to buy one from me? This is not for me."

I wasted a few days not writing. I kept telling myself, "Maybe that's a sign it wasn't meant to be. Maybe I'm not

I came. I saw. I jumped!

passionate about this writing stuff. What was I thinking?" I was close to pulling the plug and quitting this book project. Thankfully, I reminded myself why I was doing this project- to spread my message to others who also dare to reach for their dreams. I had amazing support from my wife, my family, my friends, my mentor and coach to guide me through and to cheer me on.

My story is still unfolding, but I'm living my purpose and loving every minute of it. This book is the evidence. Every day I do what I love. Having a coach has changed my life, where my results have come faster than if I was doing things on my own.

Today, I still have a coach that I meet with regularly because my coach is so valuable to me. I have become a coach myself to give back and to help others achieve their career or life goals. Every day I feel so honored to be a part of the transformational journeys of other people. There is still more to come. I like my life right now.

Stay tuned, follow my blog www.petroseshetu.com for the next interesting passion I want to pursue because I want to live my own life.

Petros Eshetu

As I grew up, I got the idea that it is normal to dislike your job. A job is not supposed to be fun. I also believed that life was too difficult. I had the "it-is-what-it-is" concept to prevent me from making changes. My new reality is that life is what you make it. If I am passionate about life, and I work on myself consistently, if I apply my gifts in the right vehicle to serve others, I will be a success.

Numerous people have books and inventions locked up in their mind but are stuck in a boring job that's killing their creativity. My hope for this book is to be the light of encouragement and inspiration for those who want to make a change in their life. There are so many aspects of life that may require you to jump, not only in your career, but also in relationships, marriage, financial situations, health, and so much more. My mission is to help people reach their full potential, one dream at a time.

Keep changing and exploring your passions. The final chapter of your book is still unfolding.

To jump takes courage. Leaving your comfort zone is scary and often uncomfortable, but if you endure until you reach the other side, you will become a much happier person.

I came. I saw. I jumped!

What are you seeking? Right now, within the next few minutes, take an active step. Do not put this book down without taking one small active step. It's is your life. Live it!

You don't have to be great to jump, but you do have to jump to be great.

Petros Eshetu

I came. I saw. I jumped!

References

"Ralph Waldo Emerson Quotes (Author of Self-Reliance and Other Essays)." Goodreads.com. Accessed December 19, 2016. https://www.goodreads.com/author/quotes/12080.Ralph_Waldo_Emerson.

"Stephen King-A Quote from On Writing." Goodreads.com. Accessed December 19, 2016. http://www.goodreads.com/quotes/7350584-the-scariest-moment-is-always-just-before-you-start.

Euripides. BrainyQuote.com, Xplore Inc, 2016. Accessed December 19, 2016. https://www.brainyquote.com/quotes/quotes/e/euripides149011.html,

Ware, Bronnie. The Top Five Regrets of the Dying: A Life Transformed by the Dearly Departing. Carlsbad, CA: Hay House, 2012.

"Procrastination (Wayne Dyer Quote)." Proverbia.net. Accessed December 19, 2016. http://en.proverbia.net/citastema.asp?tematica=949.

"Celia Cruz." Biography.com. October 12, 2015. Accessed January 2, 2017. http://www.biography.com/people/celia-cruz-40369#synopsis

"A Quote by Galileo Galilei." Goodreads. Accessed December 19, 2016. **http://www.goodreads.com/quotes/112546-passion-is-the-genesis-of-genius**

Harvey, Steve. Act like a Success, Think like a Success: Discovering Your Gift and the Way to Life's Riches. New York: Amistad, an Imprint of HarperCollinsPublishers, 2014.

J.K. Rowling's Top 10 Rules For Success. Performed by J.K. Rowling. Youtube.com. September 7, 2015. Accessed October 10, 2016. https://www.youtube.com/watch?v=bvMtUuedLwU.

"A Quote by Mark Twain." Goodreads. Accessed December 19, 2016. **http://www.goodreads.com/quotes/505050-the-two-most-important-days-in-your-life-are-the**.

Vince Lombardi. BrainyQuote.com, Xplore Inc, 2016. **https://www.brainyquote.com/quotes/quotes/v/vincelomba122285.html**, accessed December 19, 2016.

Edmund Hillary. BrainyQuote.com, Xplore Inc, 2017. **https://www.brainyquote.com/quotes/quotes/e/edmundhill104652.html**, accessed January 1, 2017.

"Quote- Vision without Action Is a Daydream. Action without Vision Is a Nightmare." Tiny Buddha (blog). Accessed December 19, 2016. **http://tinybuddha.com/wisdom-quotes/vision-without-action-is-a-daydream-action-without-vision-is-a-nightmare/**.

I came. I saw. I jumped!

"Jeff Bezos." Biography.com. July 18, 2016. Accessed December 19, 2016. http://www.biography.com/people/jeff-bezos-9542209#pioneering-e-commerce.

Carroll, Rory. "'We Need Human Interaction': Meet the LA Man Who Walks People for a Living." Half Full: Solutions, Innovations, Answers. September 14, 2016. Accessed December 19, 2016. https://www.theguardian.com/us-news/2016/sep/14/los-angeles-people-walker-chuck-mccarthy.

"The Dream Is Free, But The Hustle Is Sold Separately." The Daily Quotes. August 23, 2015. Accessed December 19, 2016. http://thedailyquotes.com/the-dream-is-free/.

Schwabel, Dan. "10 Memorable Quotes From The Start-up of YOU." Forbes. February 14, 2012. Accessed December 19, 2016. http://www.forbes.com/sites/danschawbel/2012/02/14/10-memorable-quotes-from-the-start-up-of-you/#17c432047ecf.

Lao Tzu. BrainyQuote.com, Xplore Inc, 2016. https://www.brainyquote.com/quotes/quotes/l/laotzu137141.html, accessed December 19, 2016.

"The Legend of Cliff Young: The 61 Year Old Farmer Who Won the World's Toughest Race." The Legend of Cliff Young: The 61 Year Old Farmer Who Won the World's Toughest Race. Accessed December 19, 2016. http://www.elitefeet.com/the-legend-of-cliff-young.

"The Hardest Prison To Escape is Your Mind." Famous Quotes and Sayings by Popular Authors Quoteswave. Accessed December 19, 2016.
http://www.quoteswave.com/picture-quotes/392063.

Tracy, Brian. "Understanding Your Subconscious Mind." Brian Tracy's Blog (blog), September 15, 2016. Accessed December 19, 2016.
http://www.briantracy.com/blog/general/understanding-your-subconscious-mind/.

Marianne Szegedy. "Mysteries Of The Mind: Your unconscious is making your everyday decisions. U.S News and World Reports (Fed 28,2005).
file:///C:/Users/Petros%20Eshetu/Downloads/95%25%20Sub%202002005%20USNews%20copy.pdf

Dyer, Wayne. "Success Secrets." Dr. Wayne W. Dyer. October 06, 2014. Accessed December 19, 2016.
http://www.drwaynedyer.com/blog/success-secrets/.

"A Quote by Confucius." Goodreads. Accessed December 19, 2016. **http://www.goodreads.com/quotes/874427-he-who-who-says-he-can-and-he-who-says.**

Dave, Mike, and Fabian. "The Holstee Manifesto." Holstee. Accessed December 19, 2016.
https://www.holstee.com/pages/manifesto

I came. I saw. I jumped!

Petros Eshetu

I came. I saw. I jumped!

About the Author

Petros Eshetu is an Ethiopian, who grew up in Harare, Zimbabwe for most of his childhood. He attended the University of Wisconsin-Eau Claire and attained a Bachelor of Business-Finance and MBA. He currently works as a personal development coach, having previously worked in corporate America for 5 years and now lives in Minneapolis with his wife Lisa.

Disillusioned with some aspects of his life, Petros decided to answer a question which had been at the centre of his thoughts for many years.

What is my passion and purpose?

Having spent many months researching, and learning from successful people, he transformed his life by applying the principles learnt, allowing himself to realize his dream of becoming a writer at the same time.

In his spare time Petros enjoys an obsession with reading and visiting book stores. He also loves to indulge himself by trying out new cafes and restaurants with Lisa, travelling the world to visit his far-flung family and friends, while exploring new places.

This is Petros' first book, but he hopes that it will be the first of many which will go some way to helping others.

Petros Eshetu

In the future he hopes to continue travelling and tick off all the places on his bucket list that he has still to visit. He is also determined to continue writing and to become an awesome coach, with the ability to help others to realise their own dreams.

Petros' favorite quote goes some way to helping with that – 'In the end, it's not the years in your life that count. It's the life in your years.' Abraham Lincloin

You can contact Petros at **petros@petroseshetu.com**. You can also stay connected with him through www.petroseshetu.com.

I came. I saw. I jumped!

www.ingramcontent.com/pod-product-compliance
Lightning Source LLC
Chambersburg PA
CBHW071455040426
42444CB00008B/1347